# Sugar Skulls - Day of The Dead

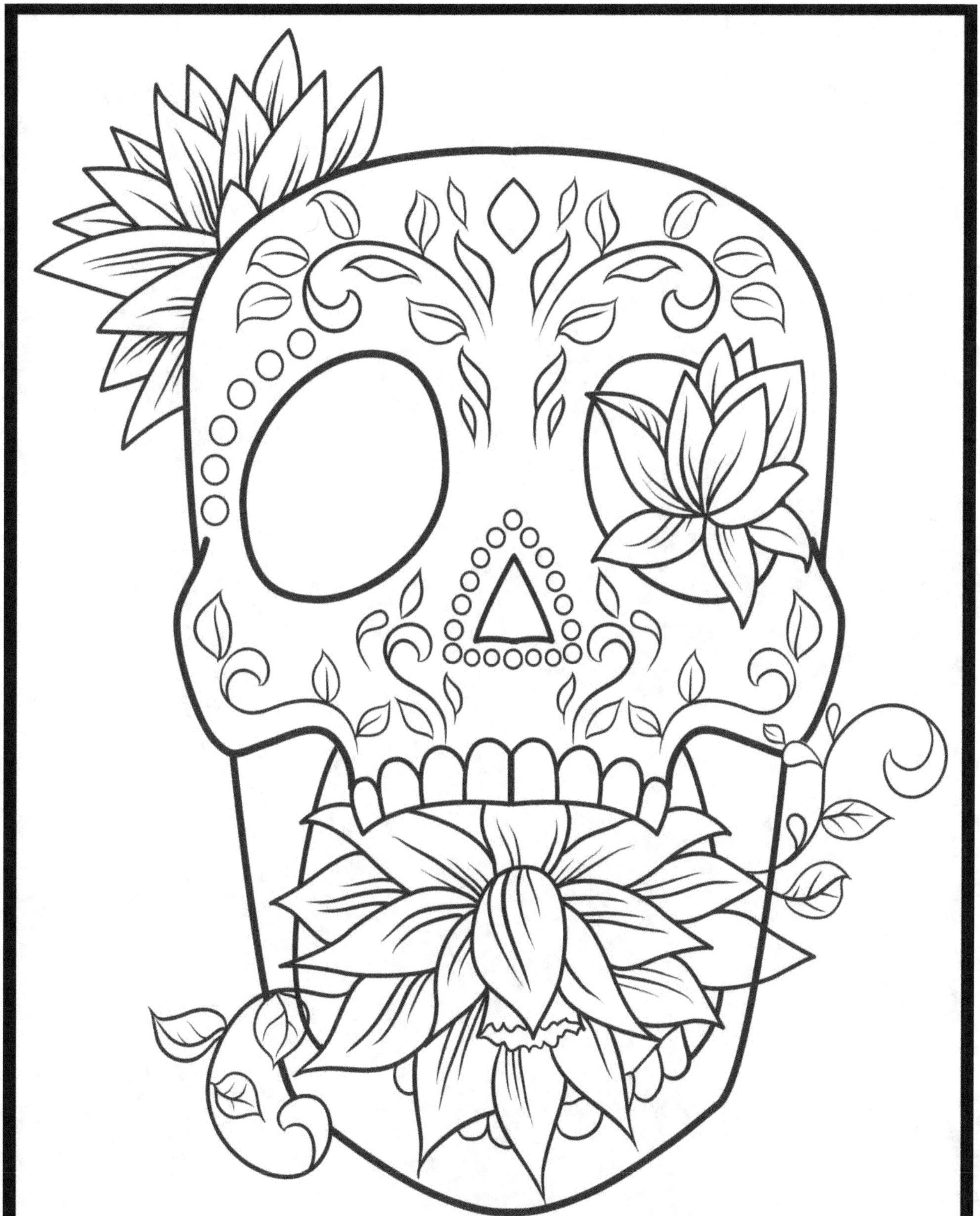

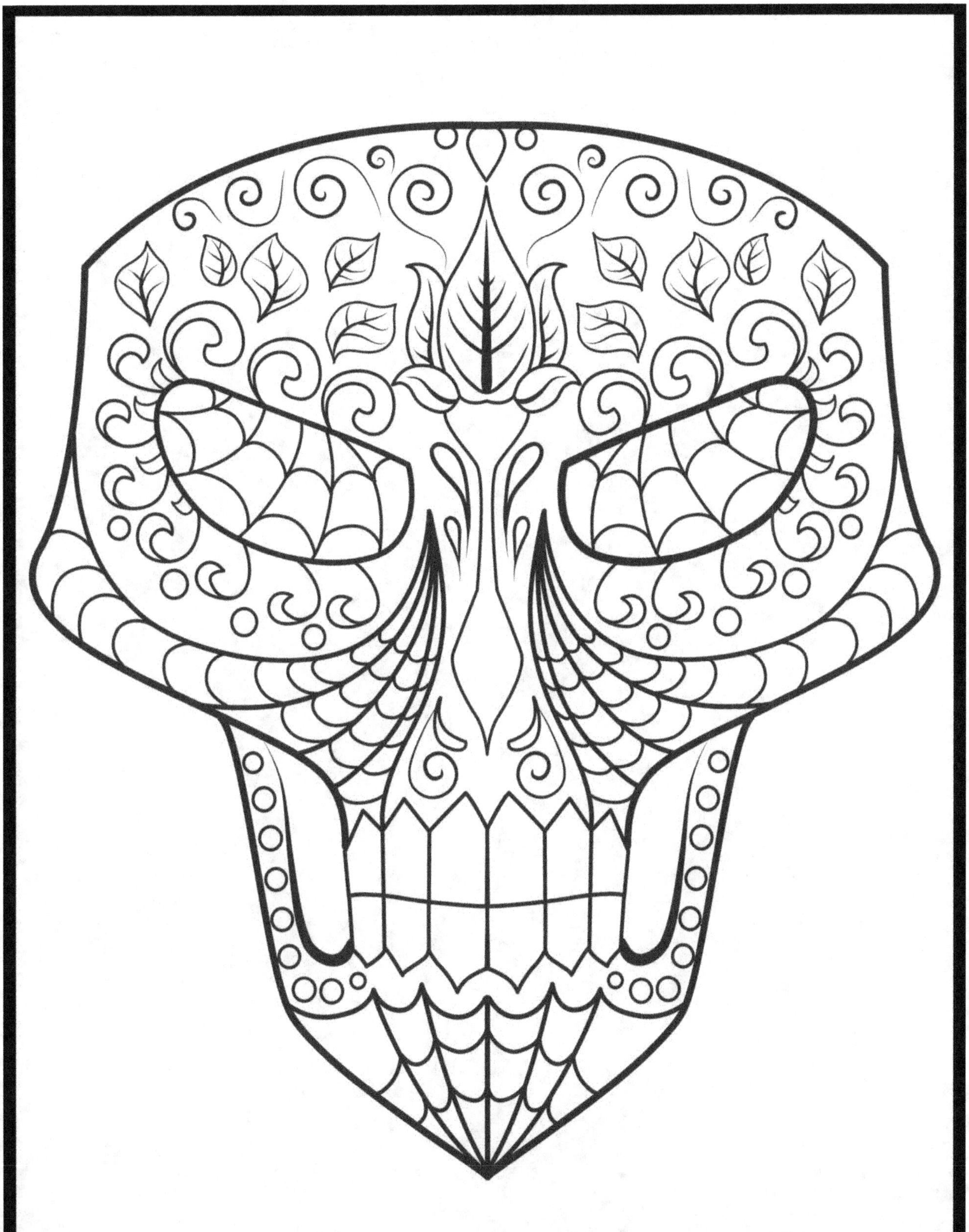

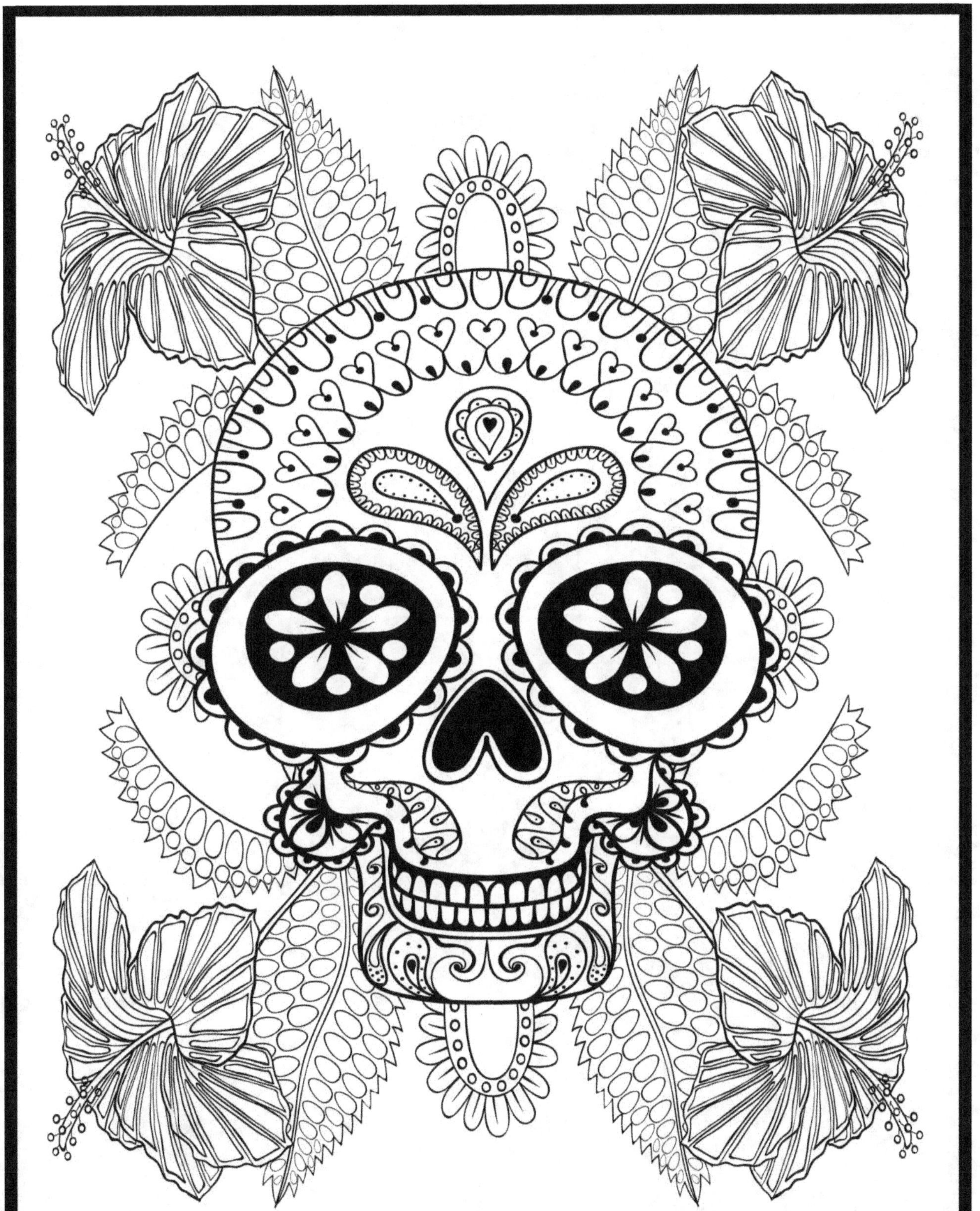

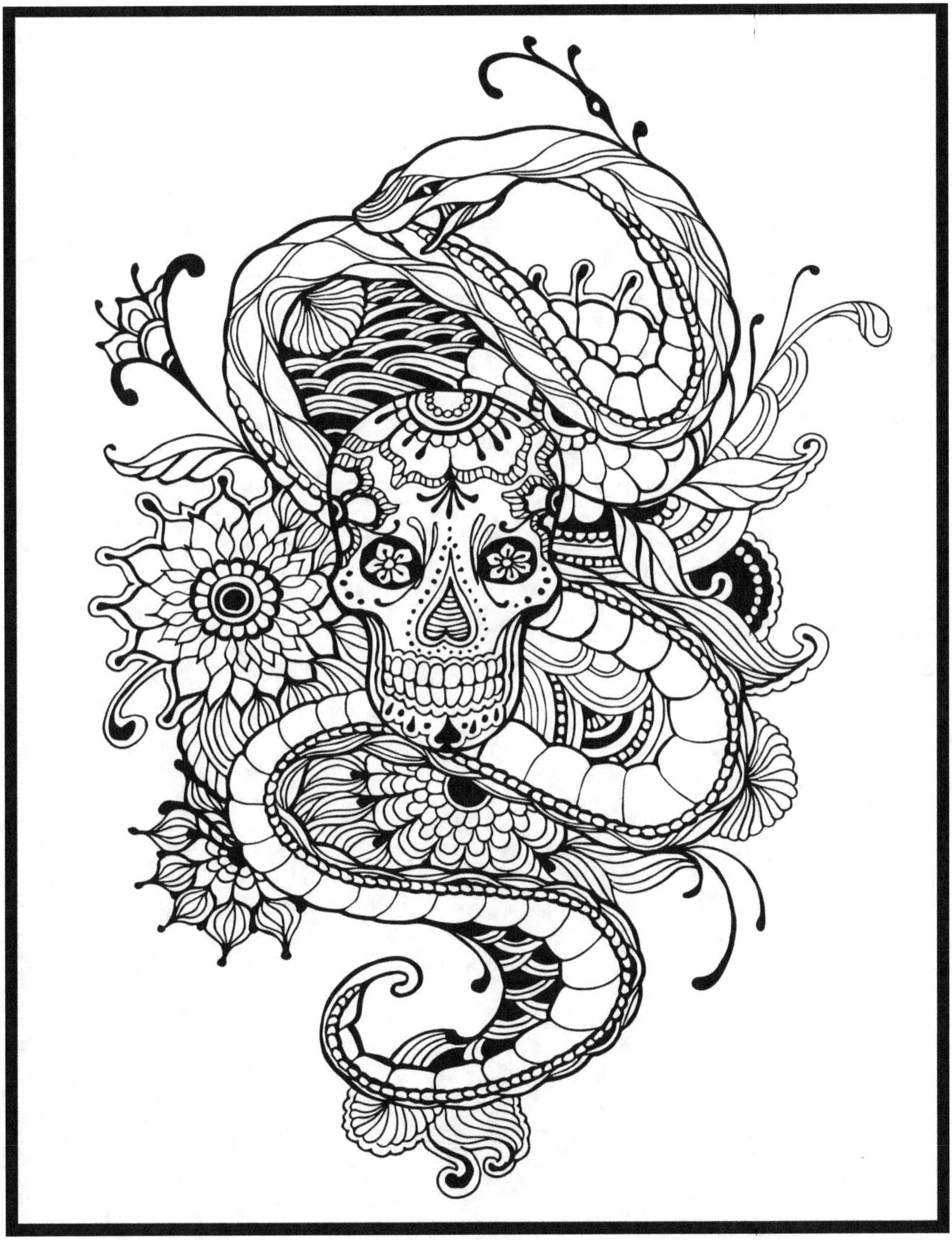

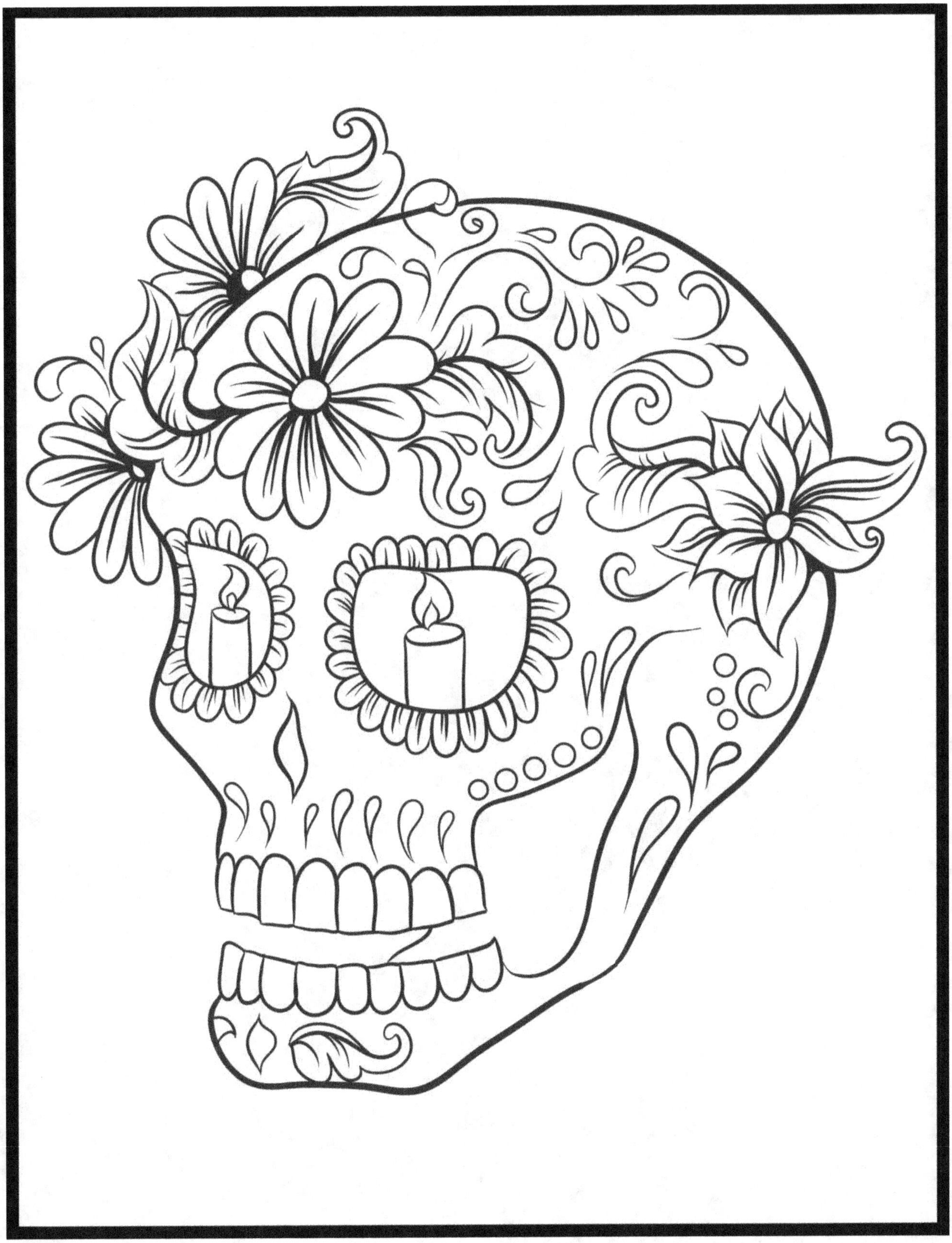

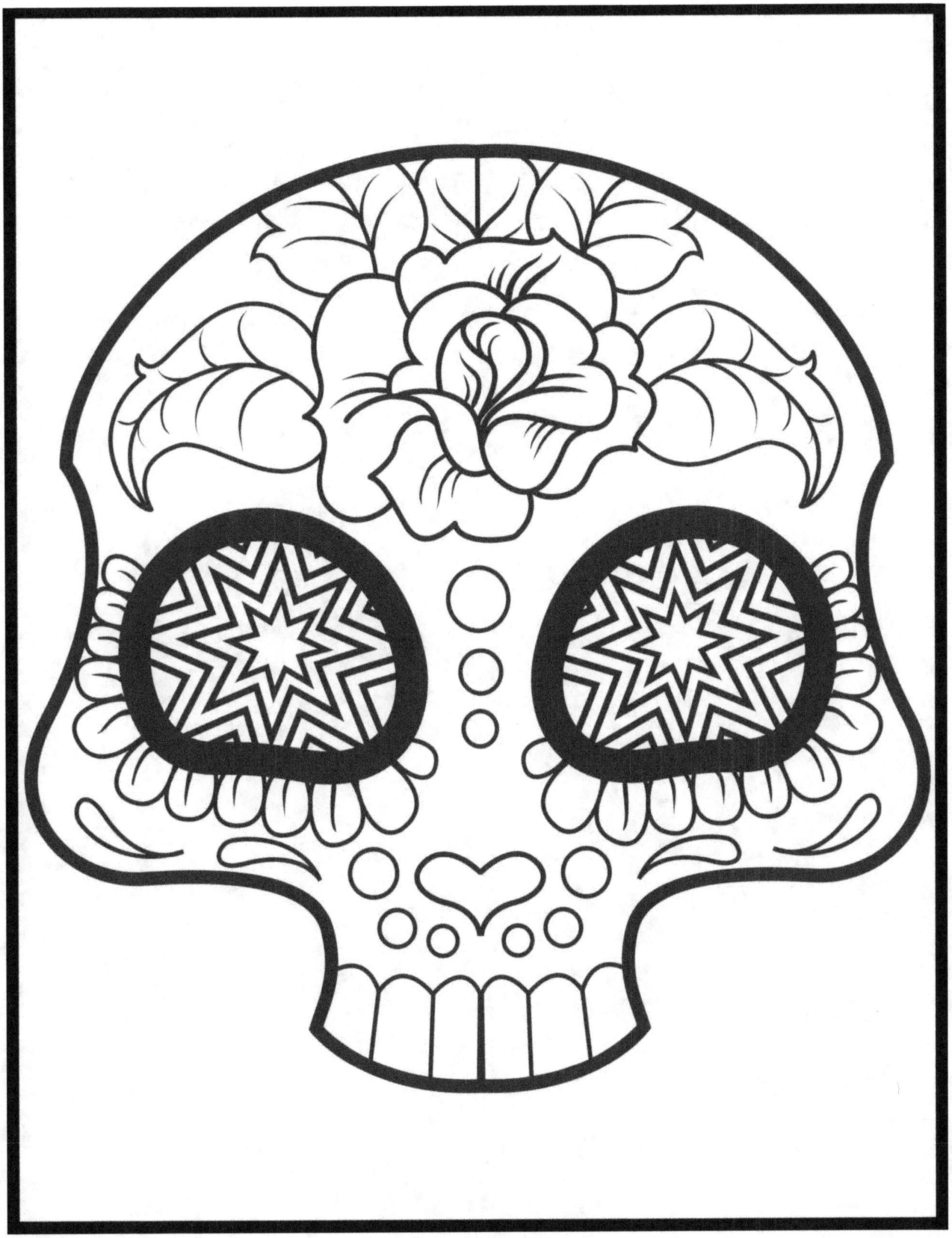

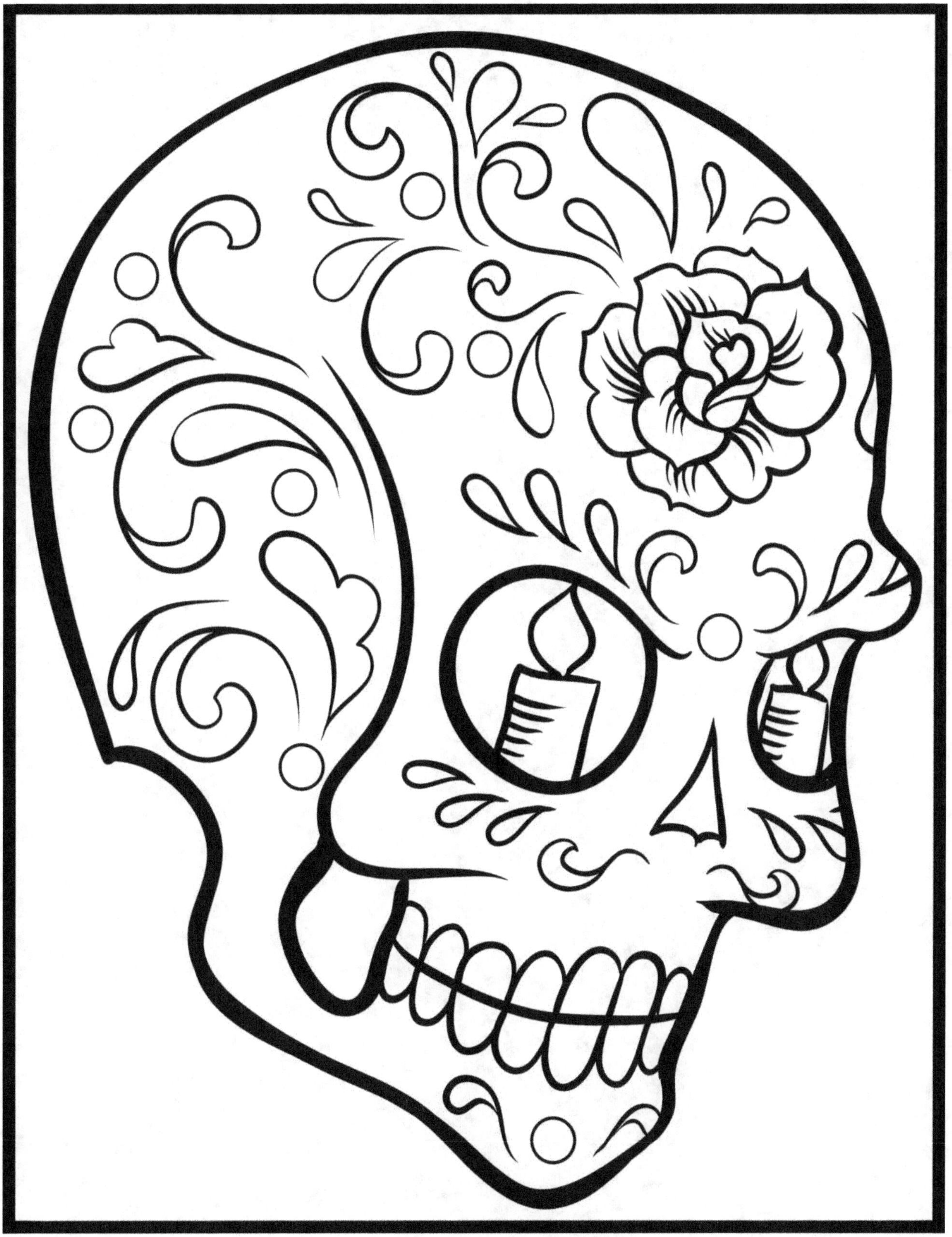

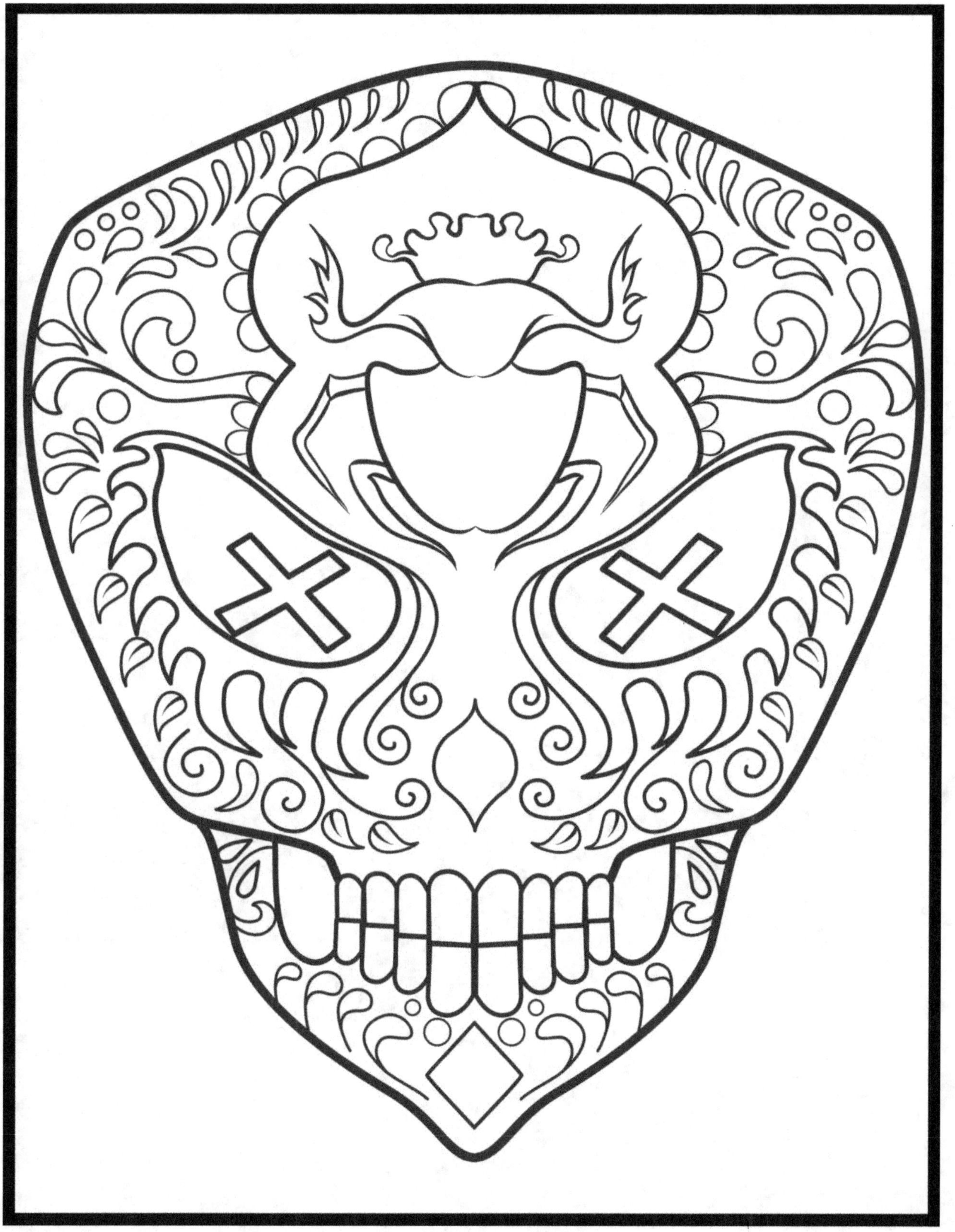

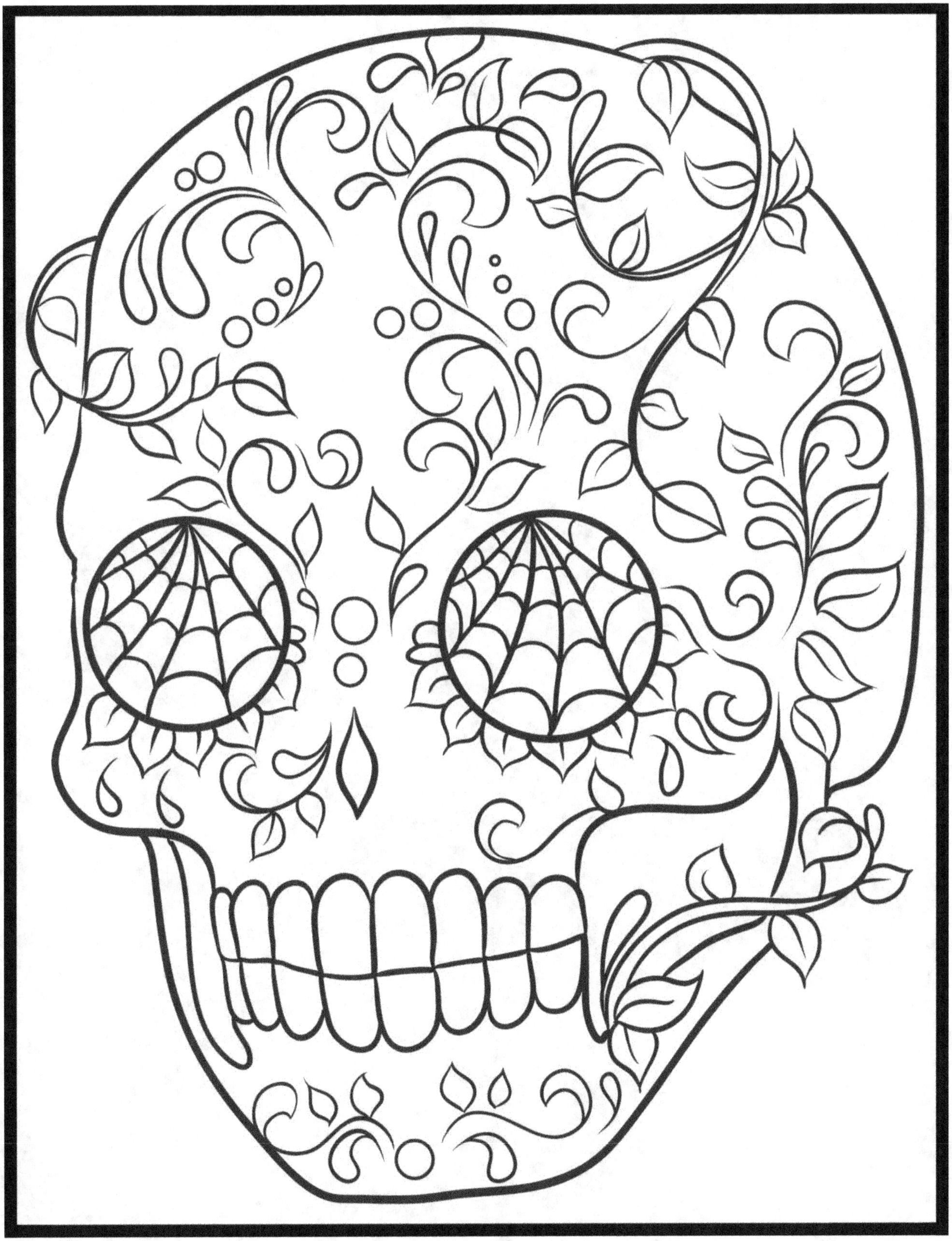

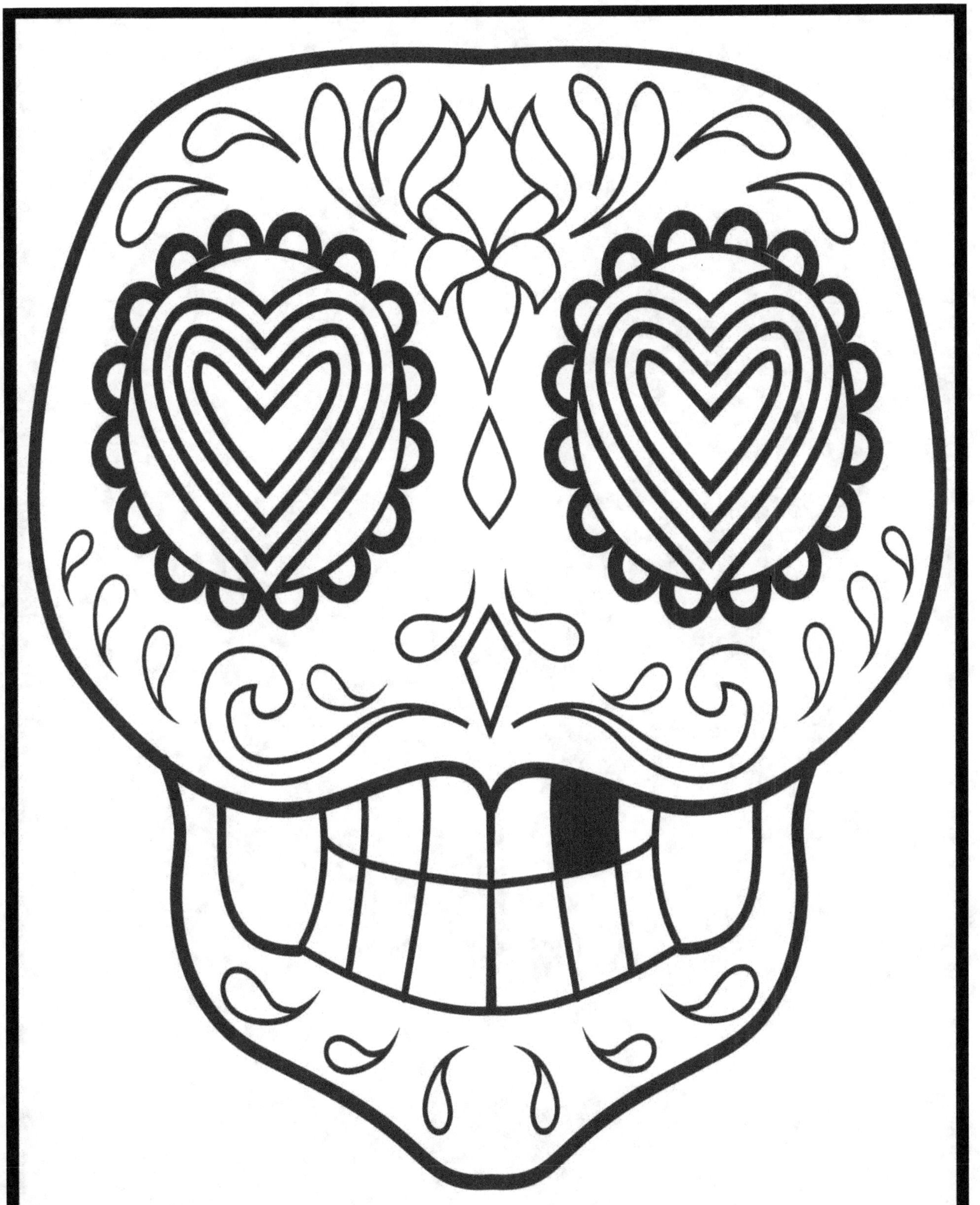

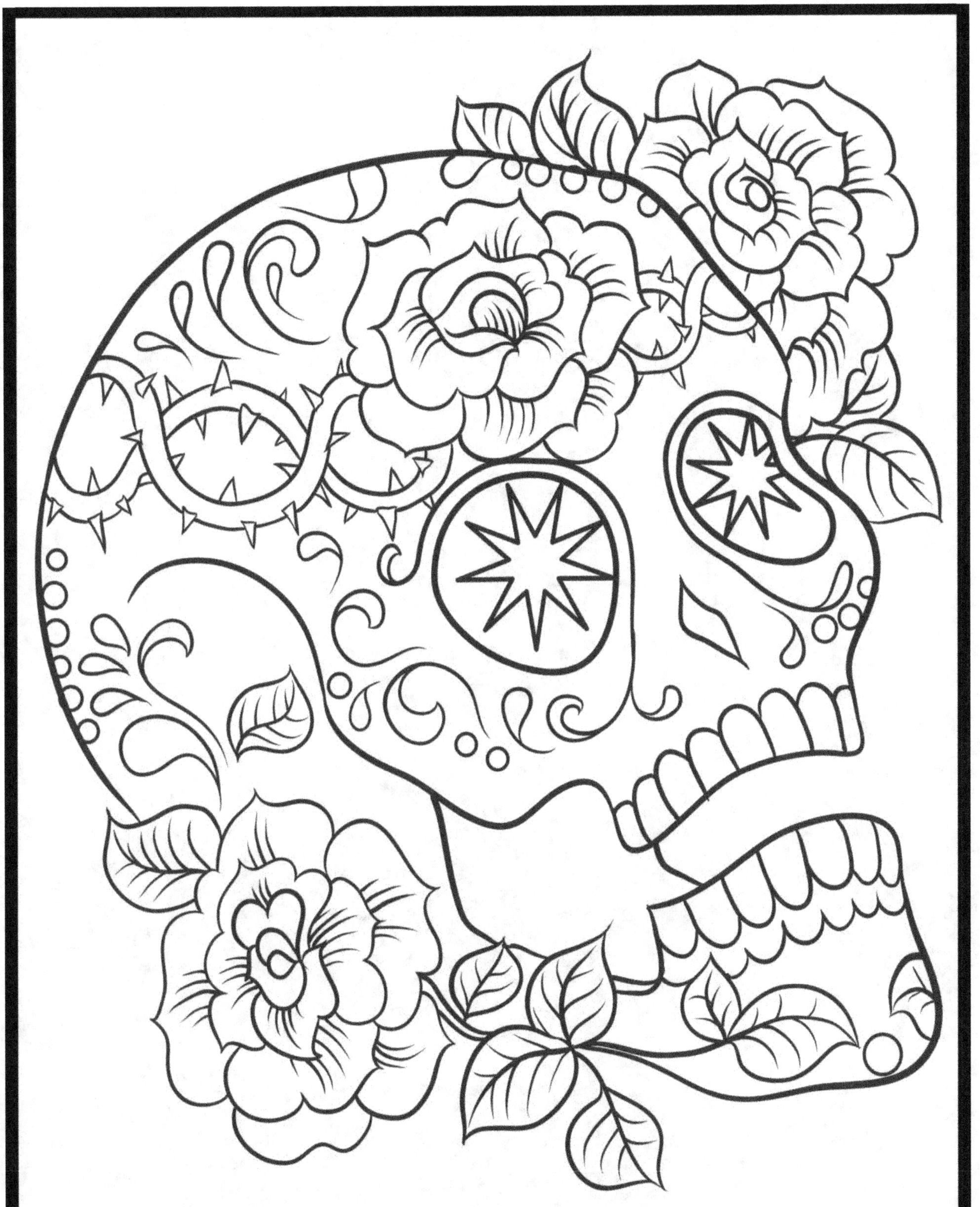

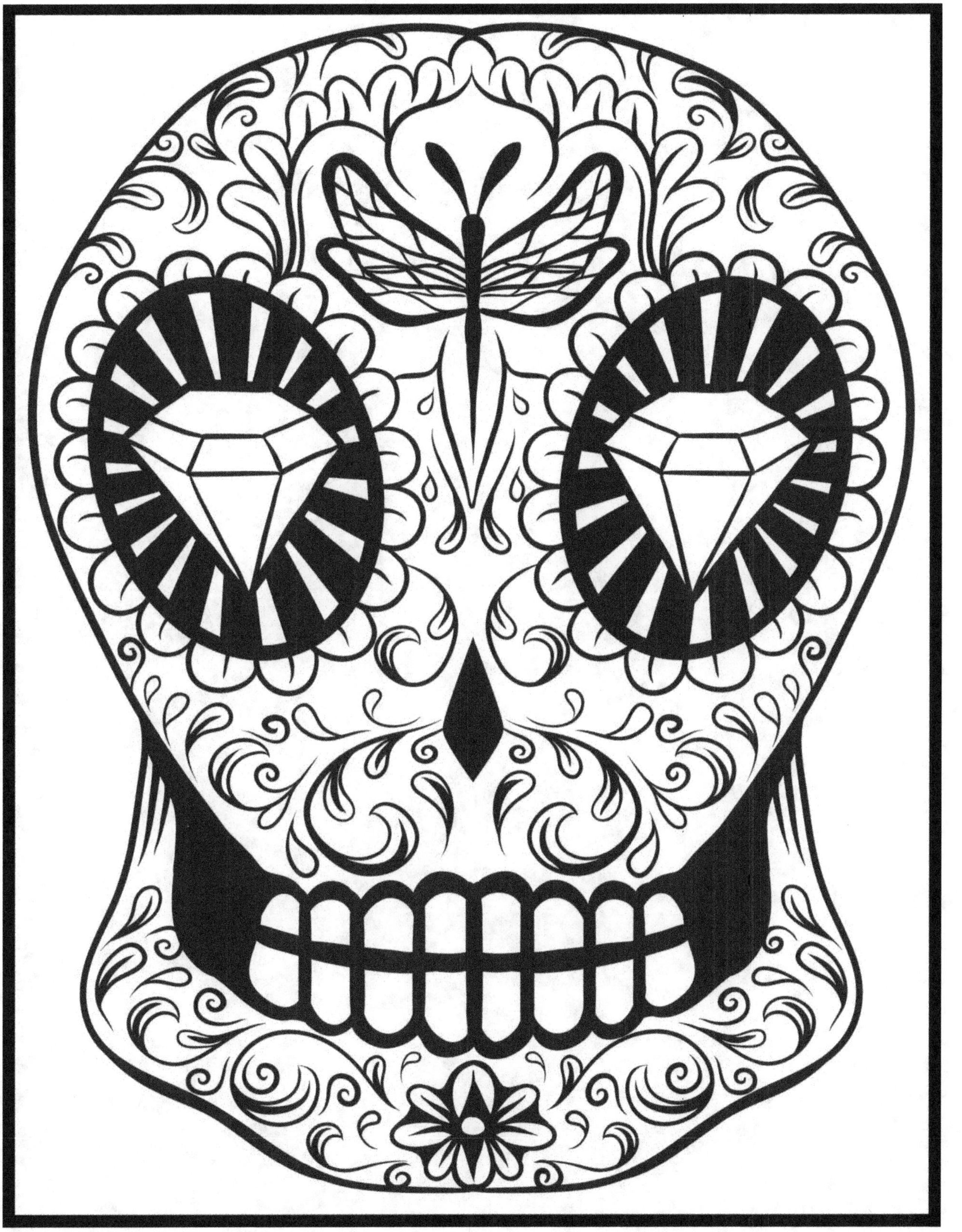

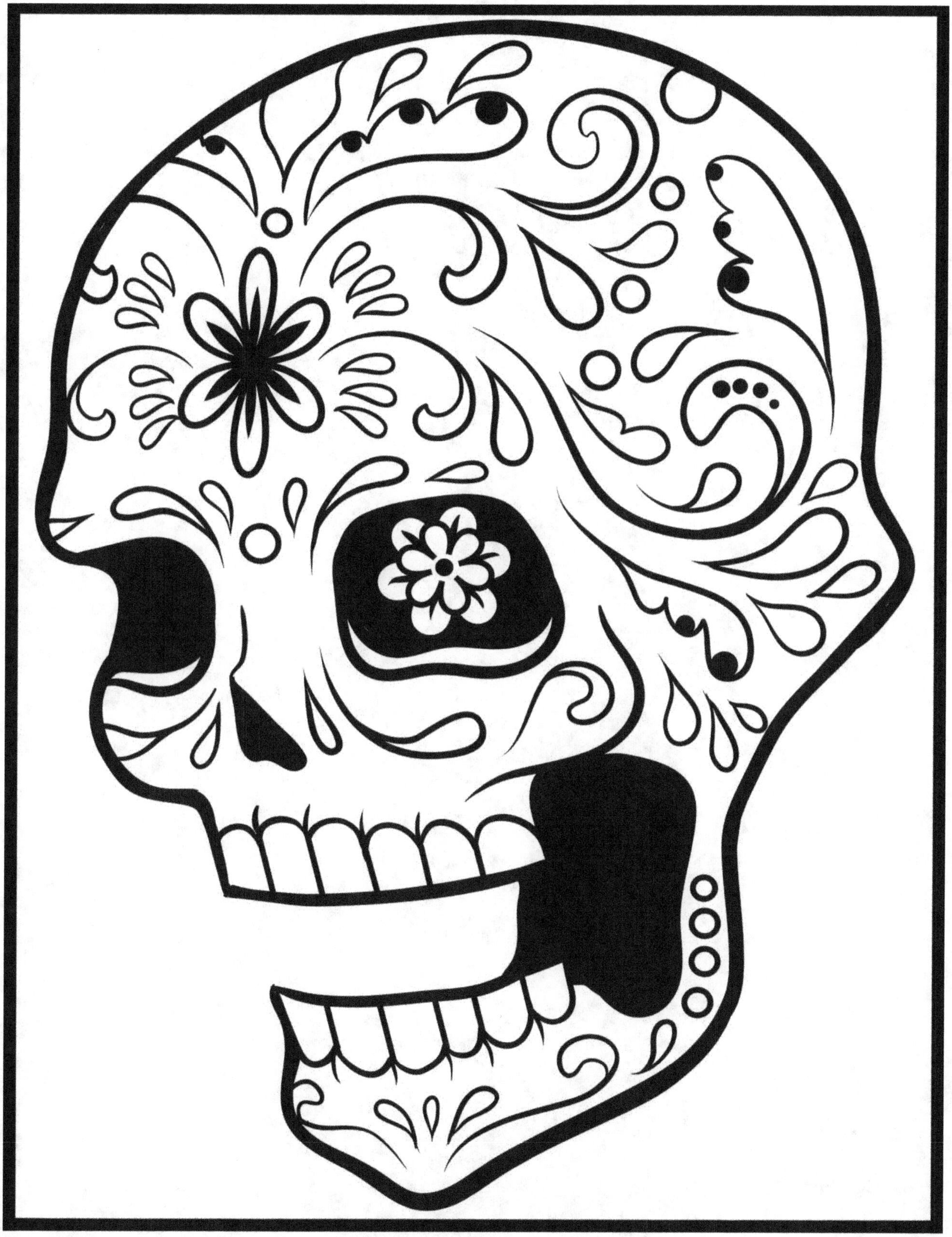

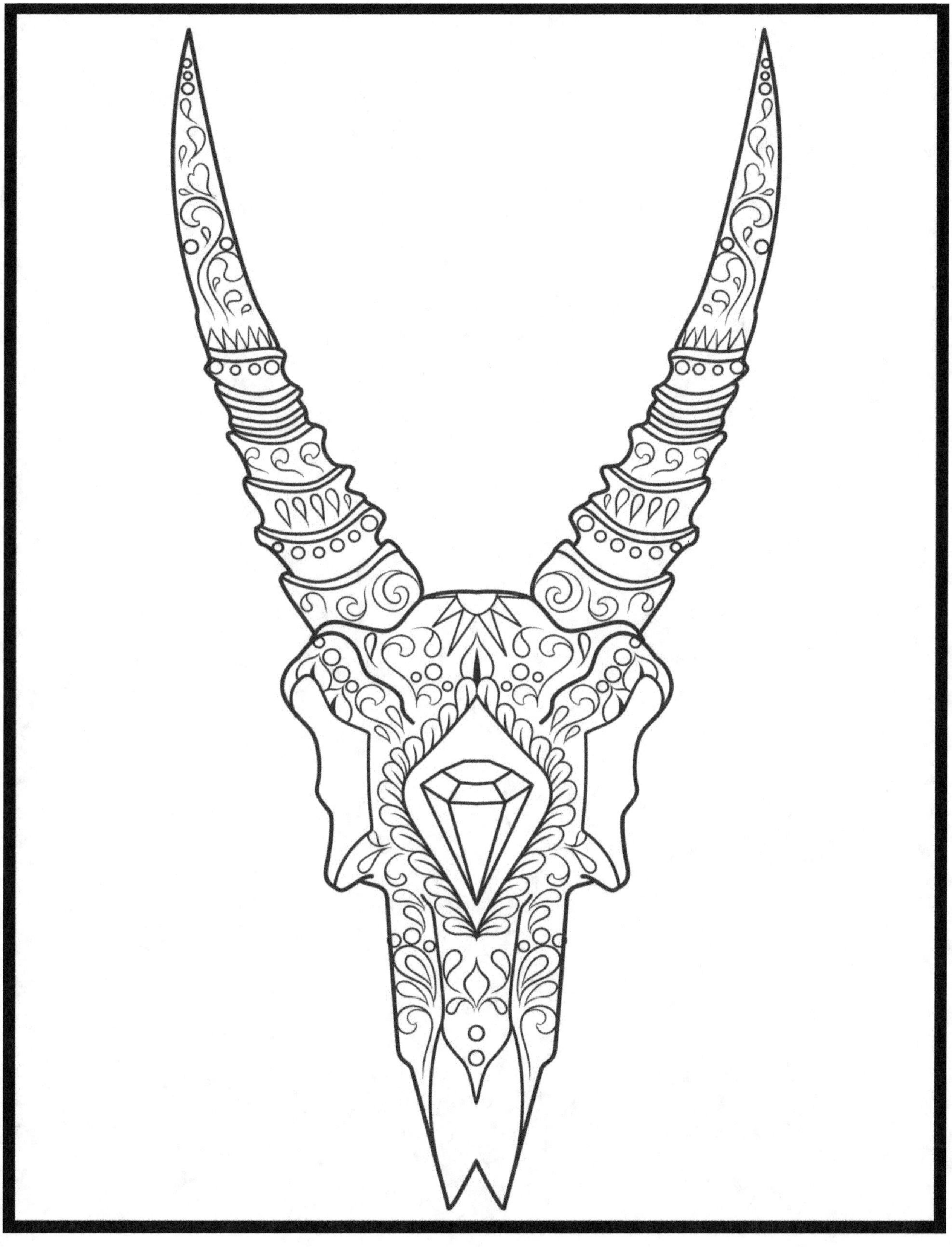

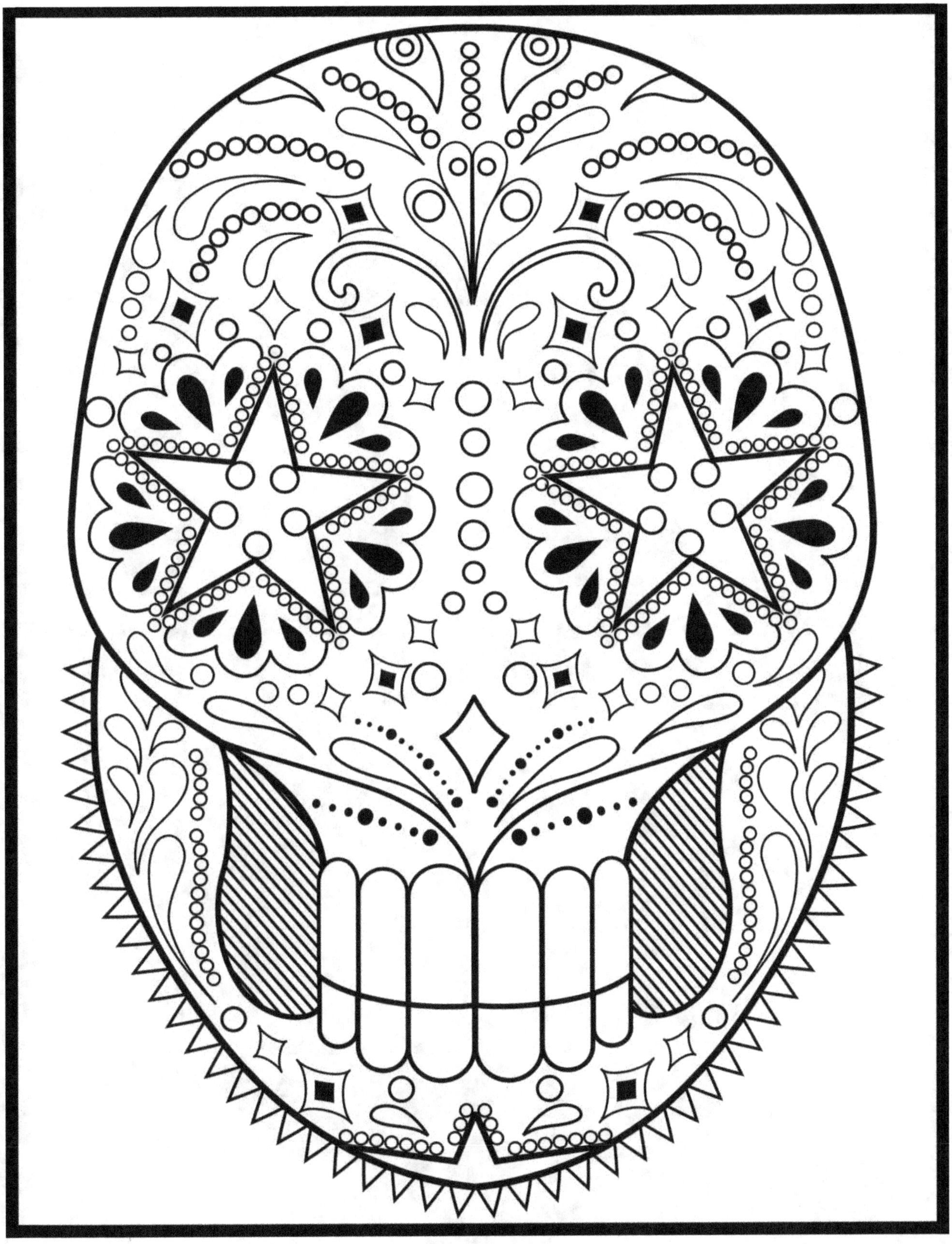

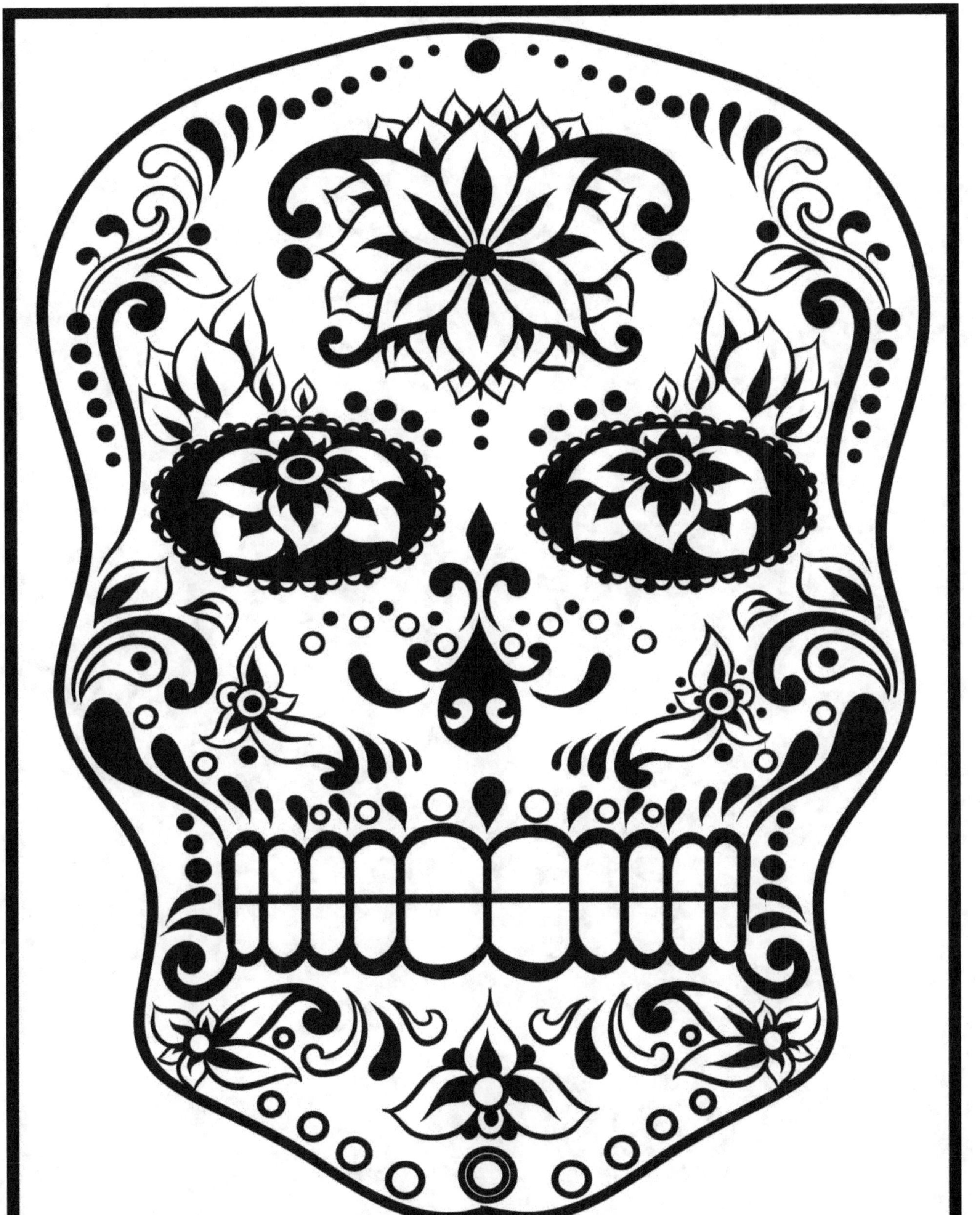

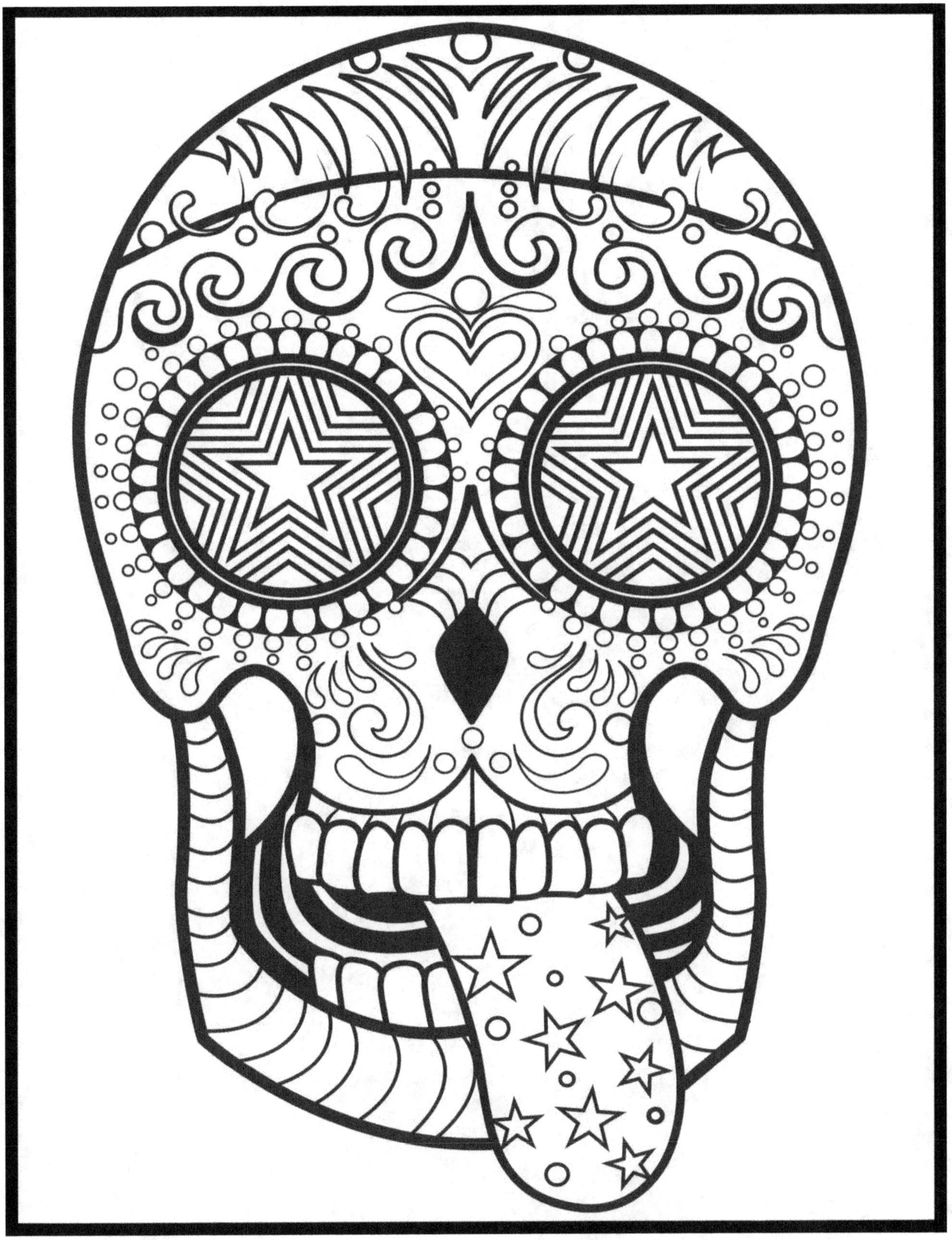

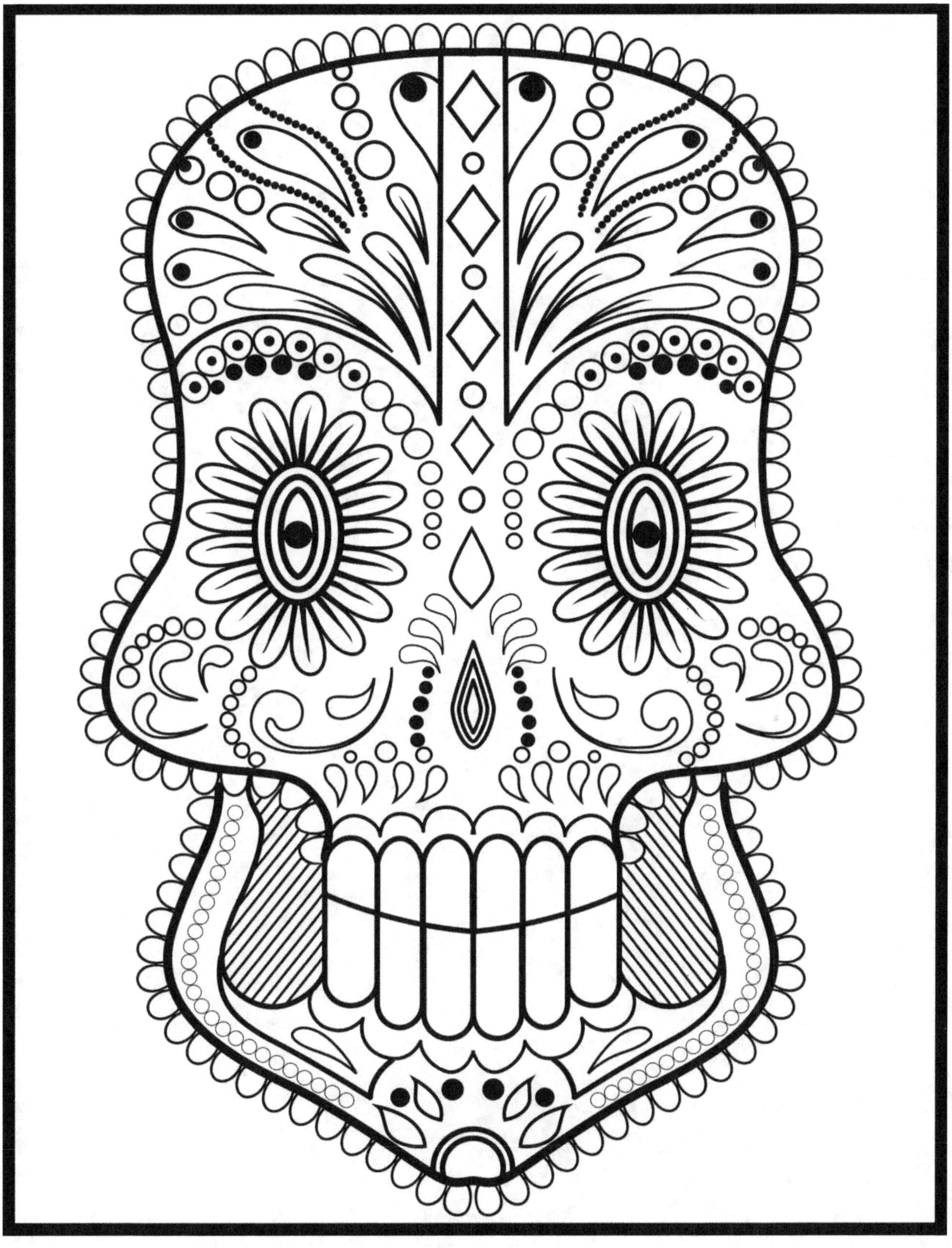

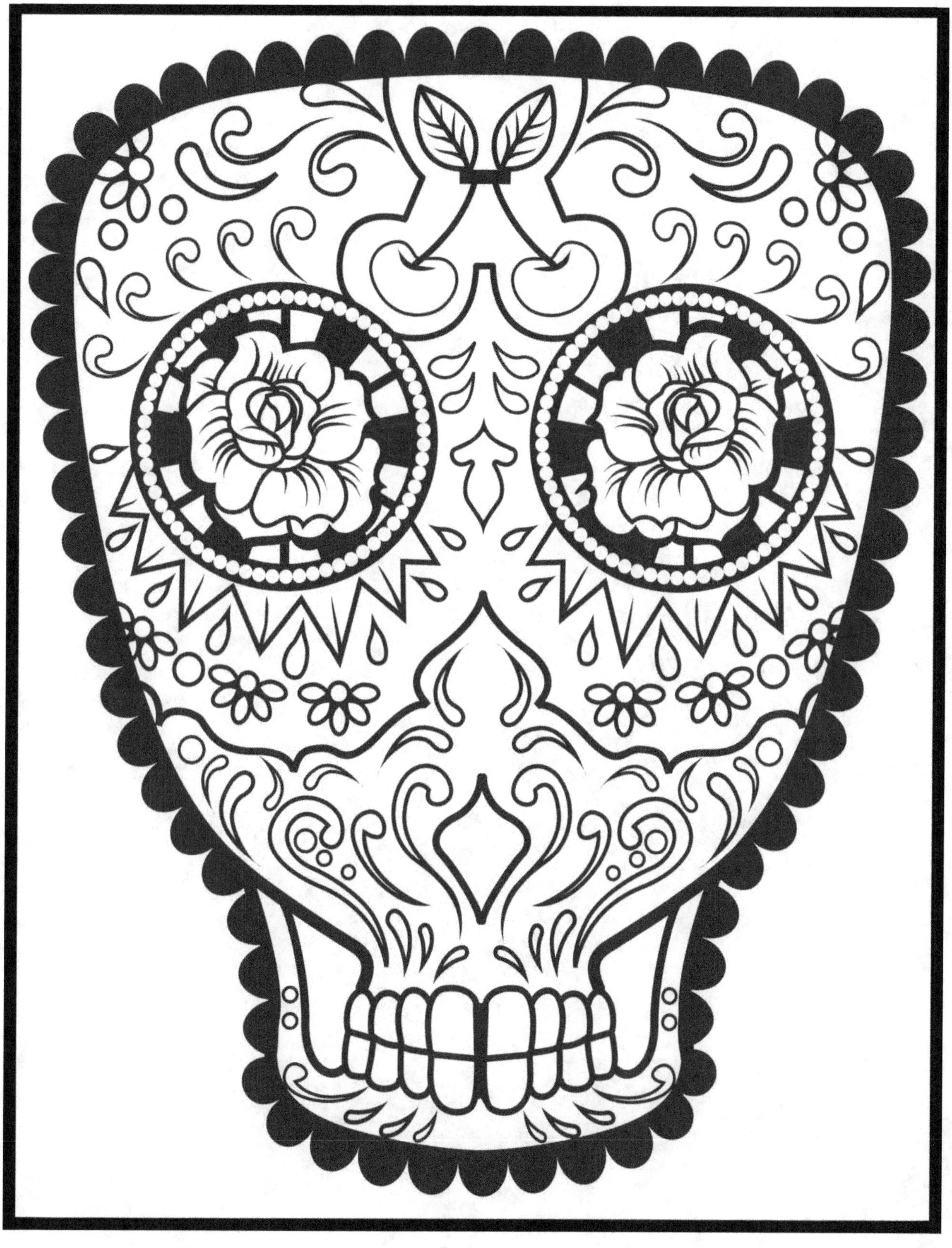

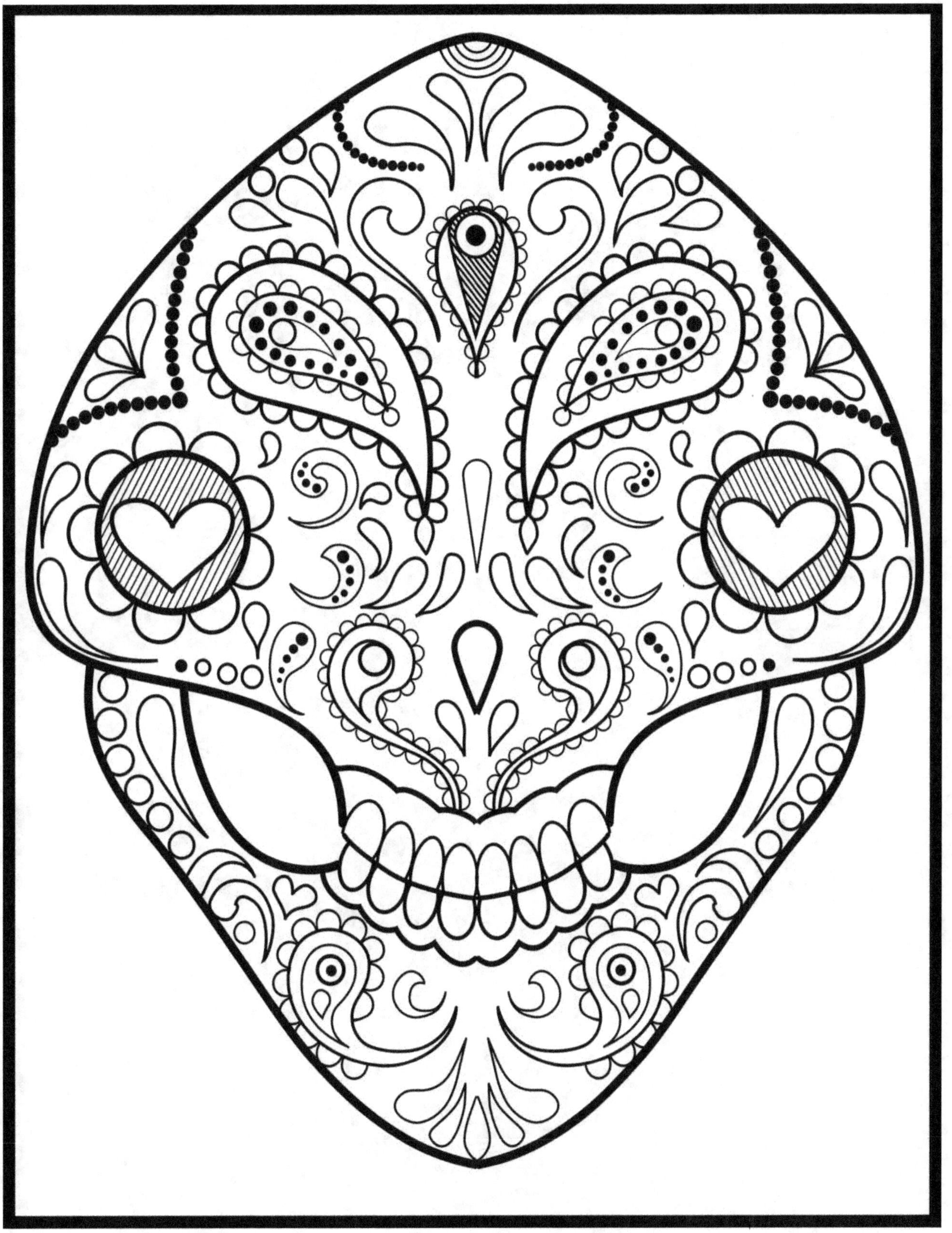

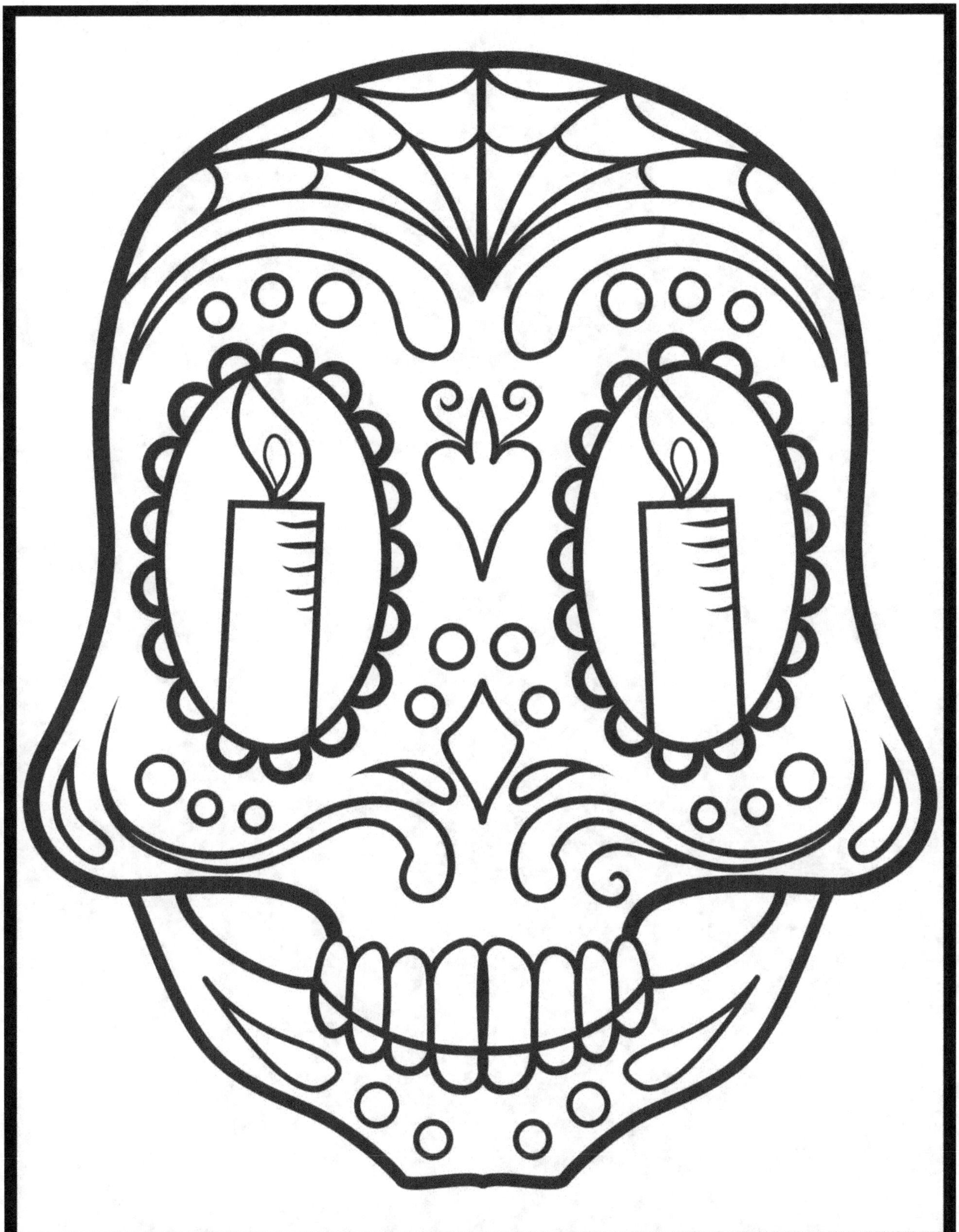

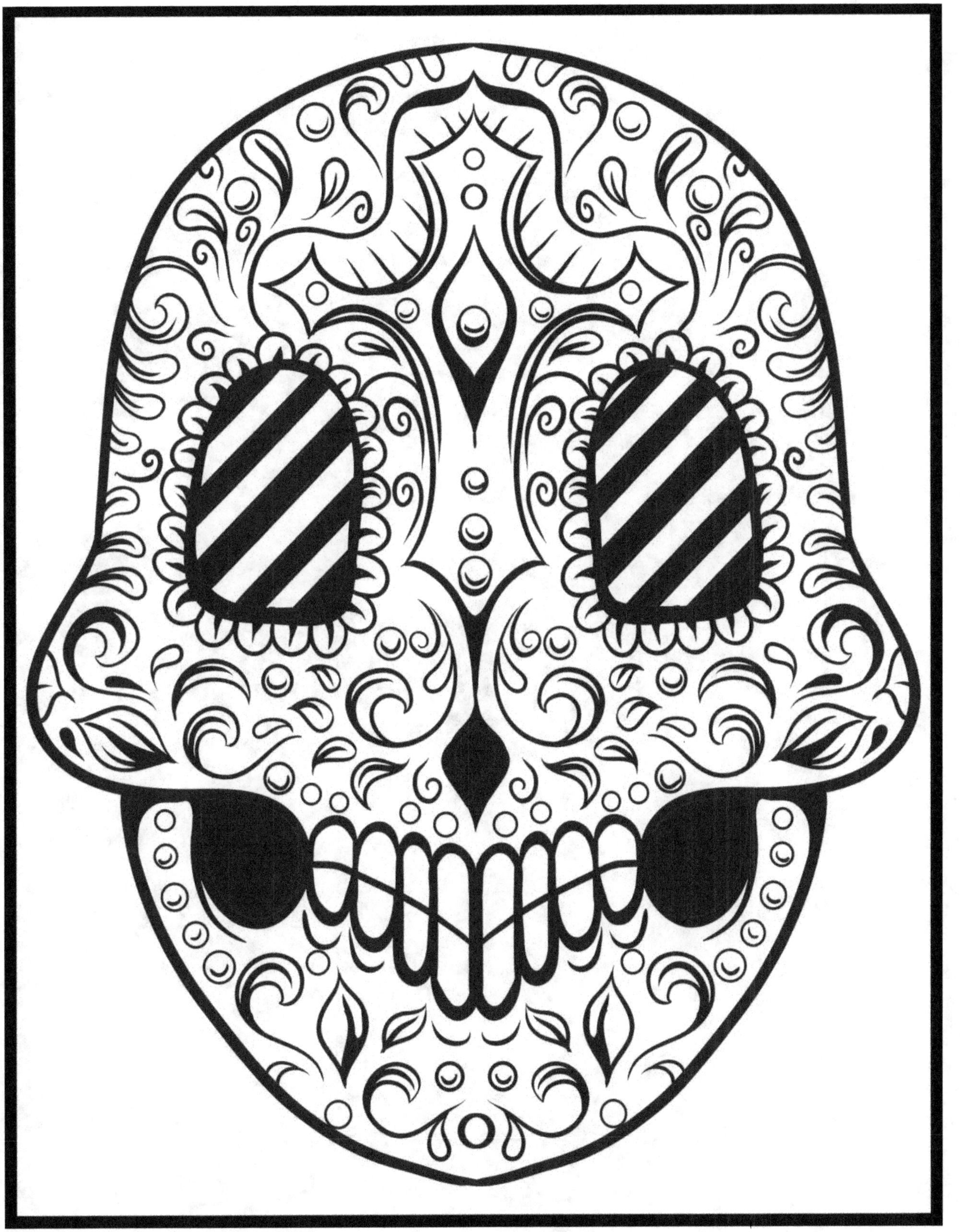

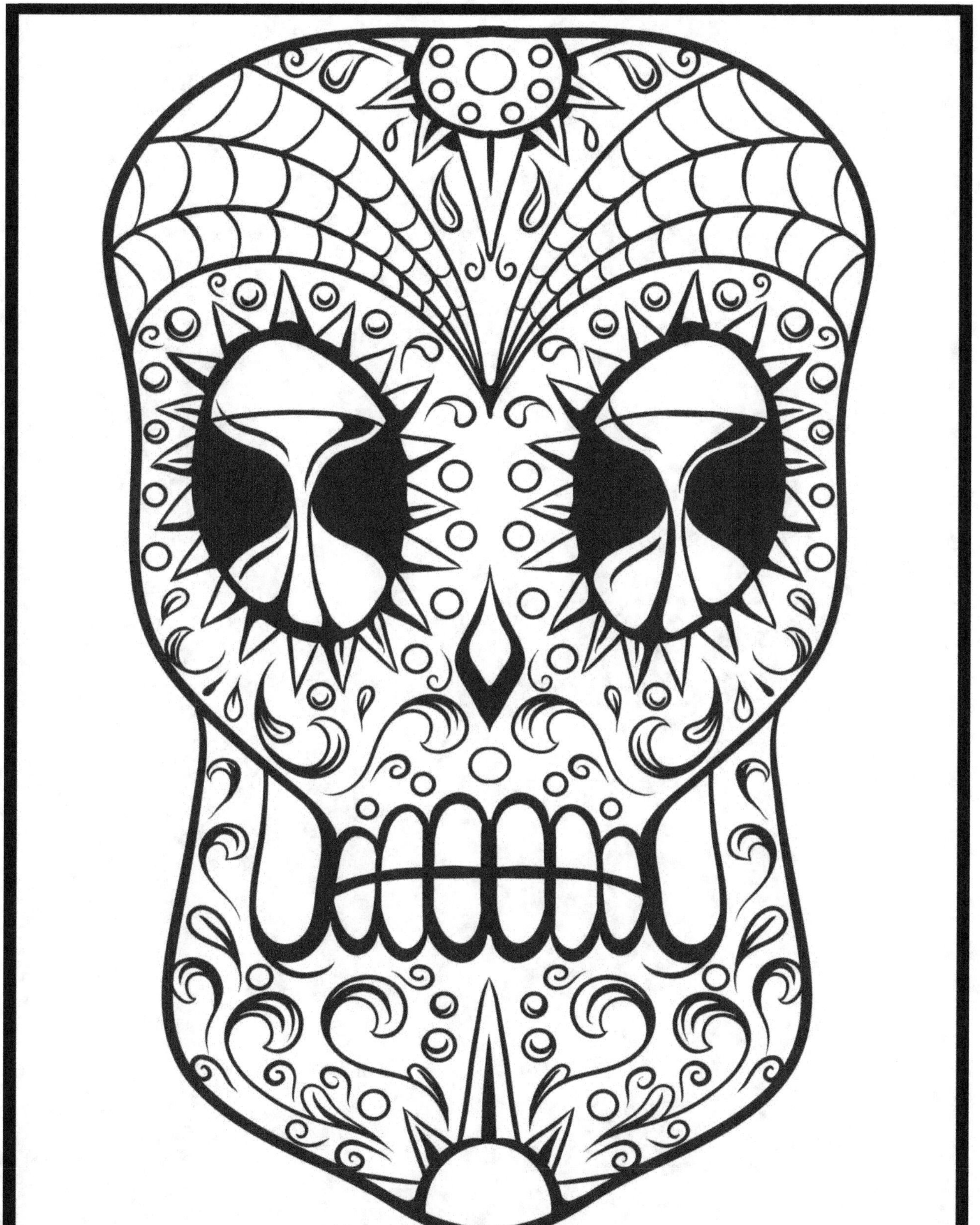

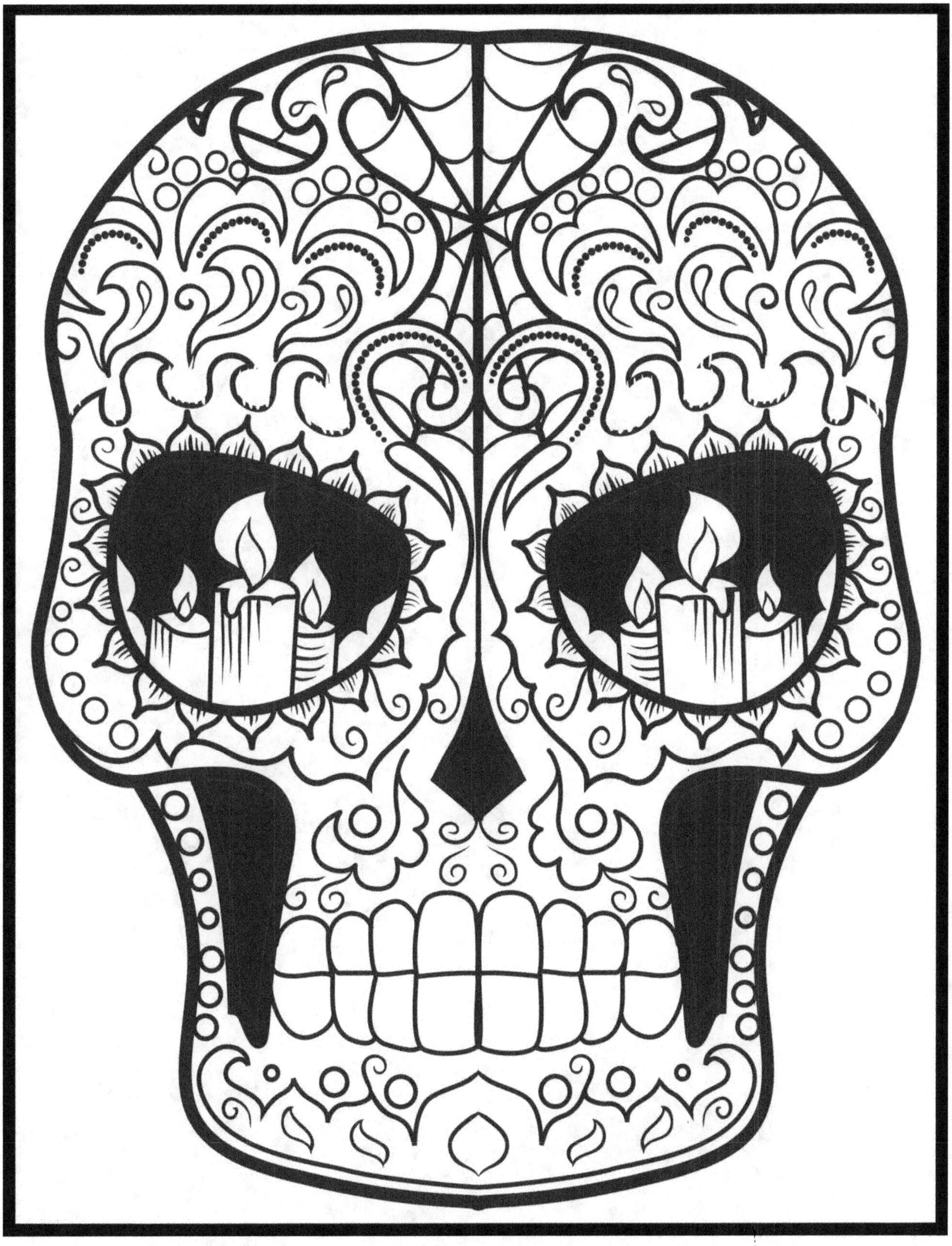

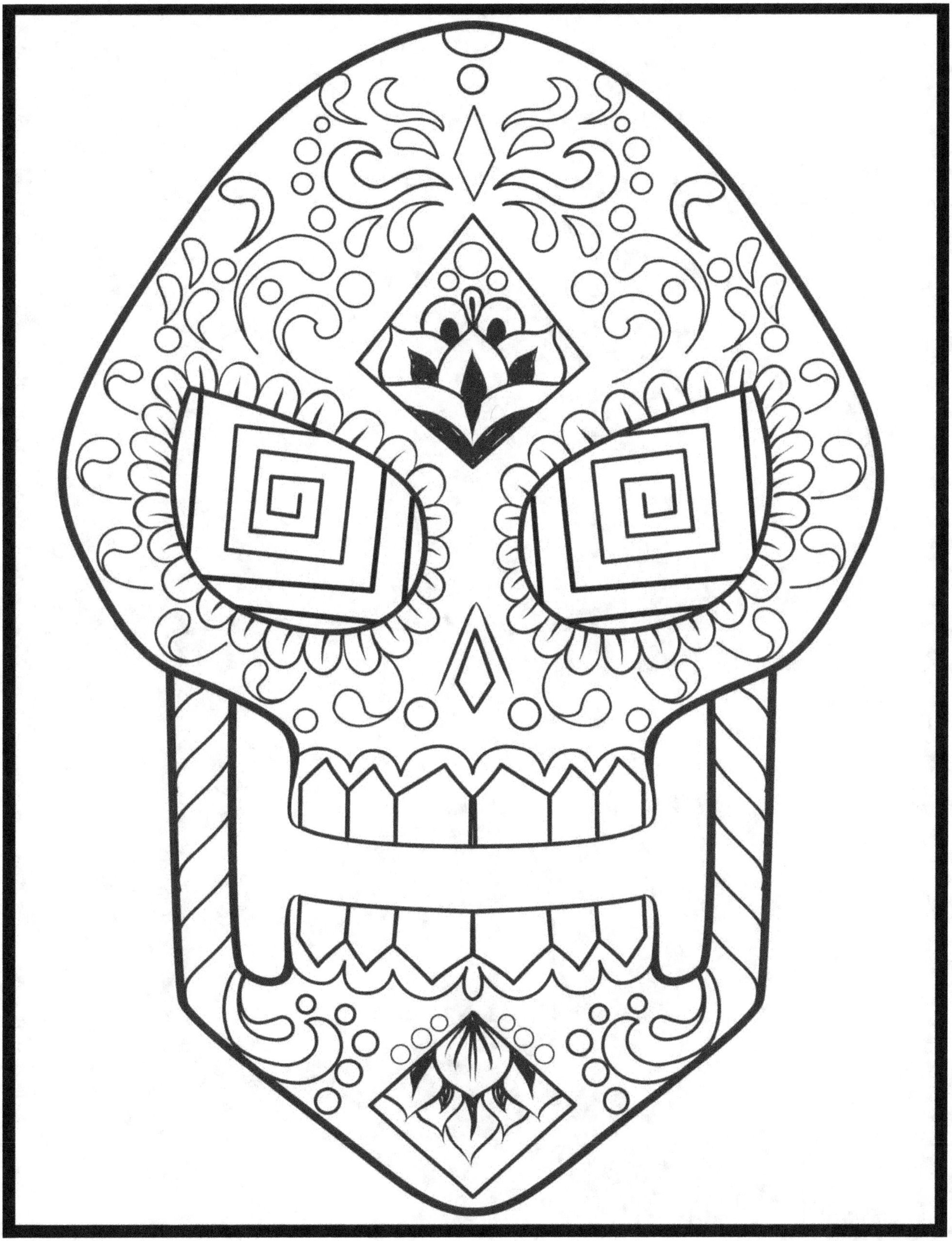

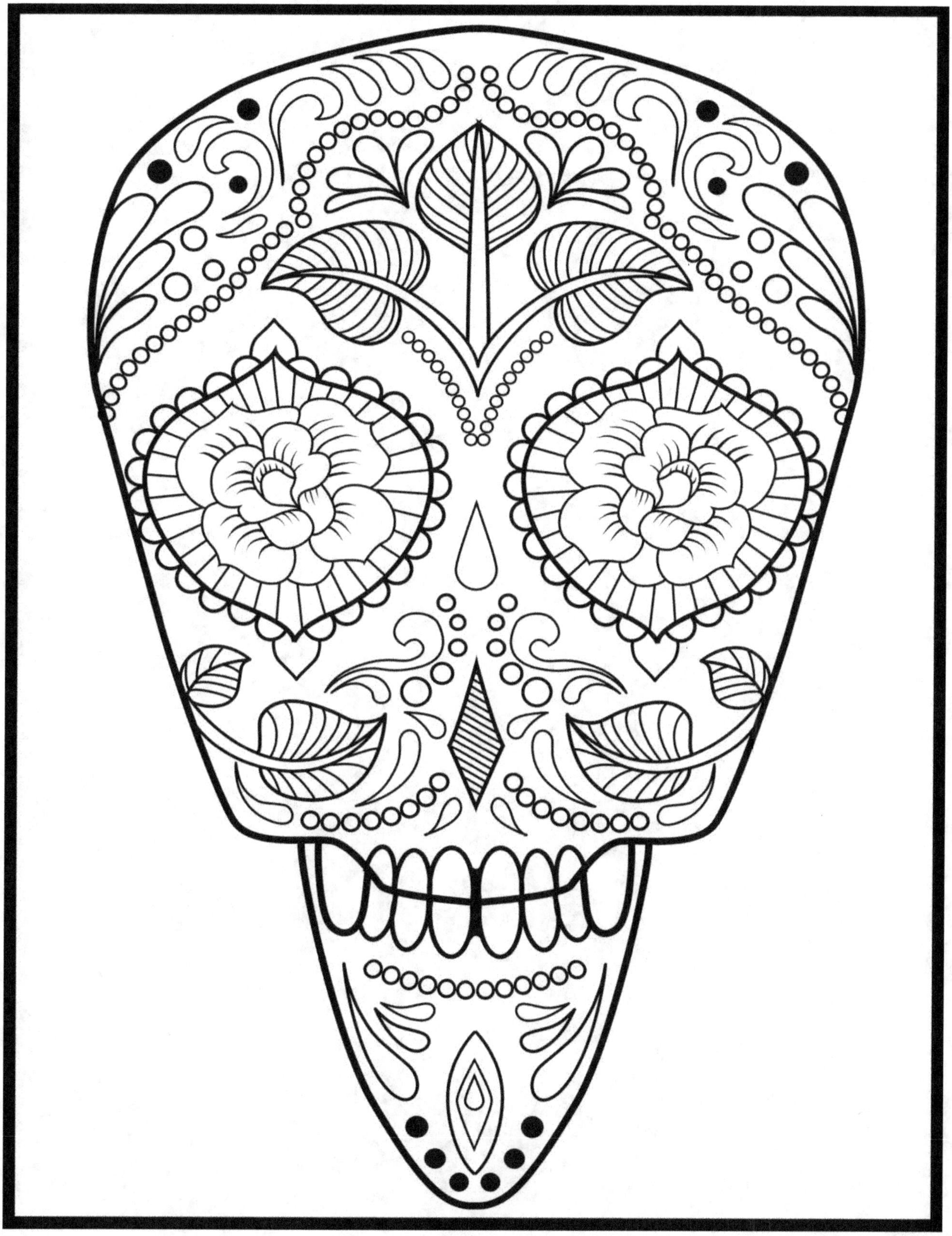

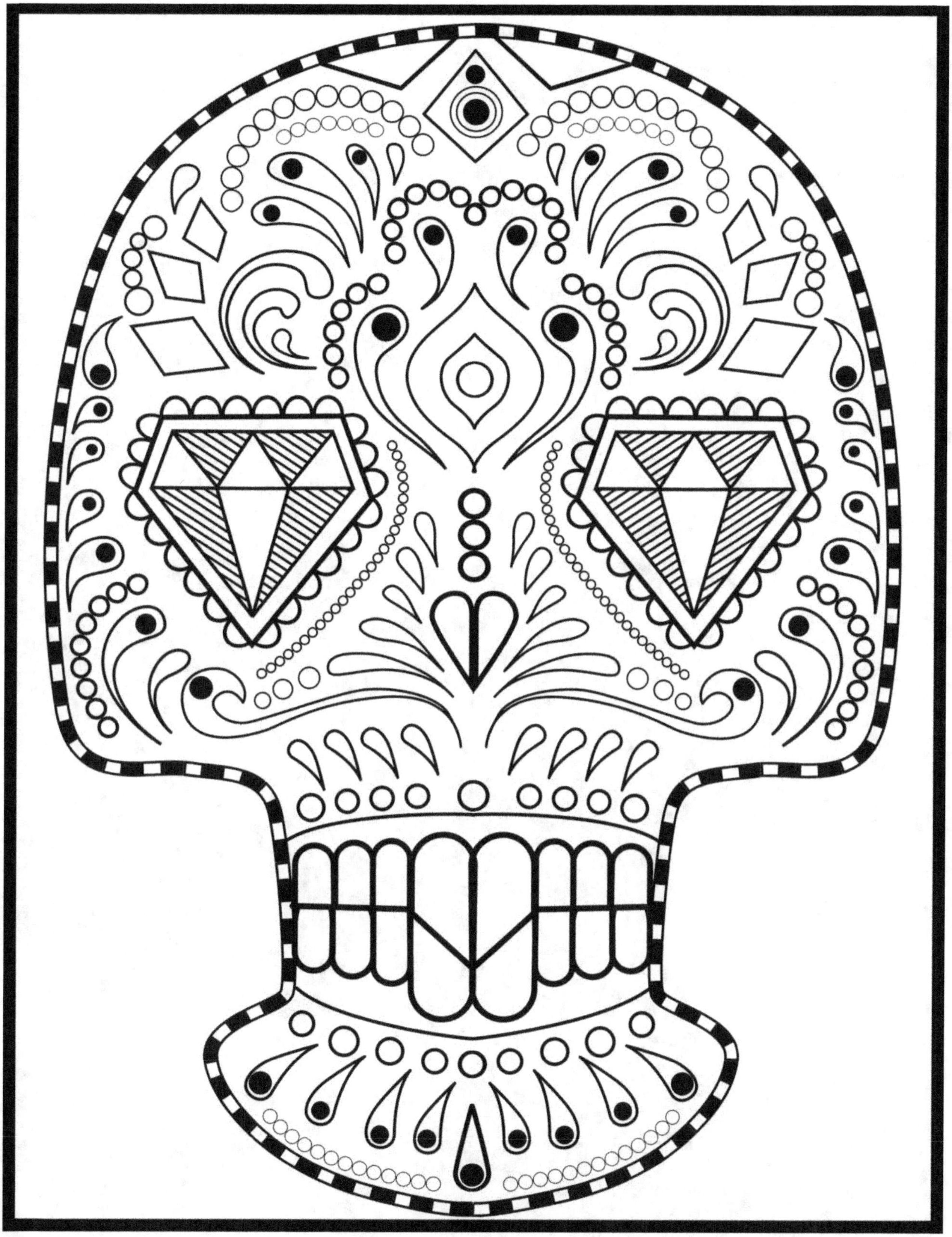

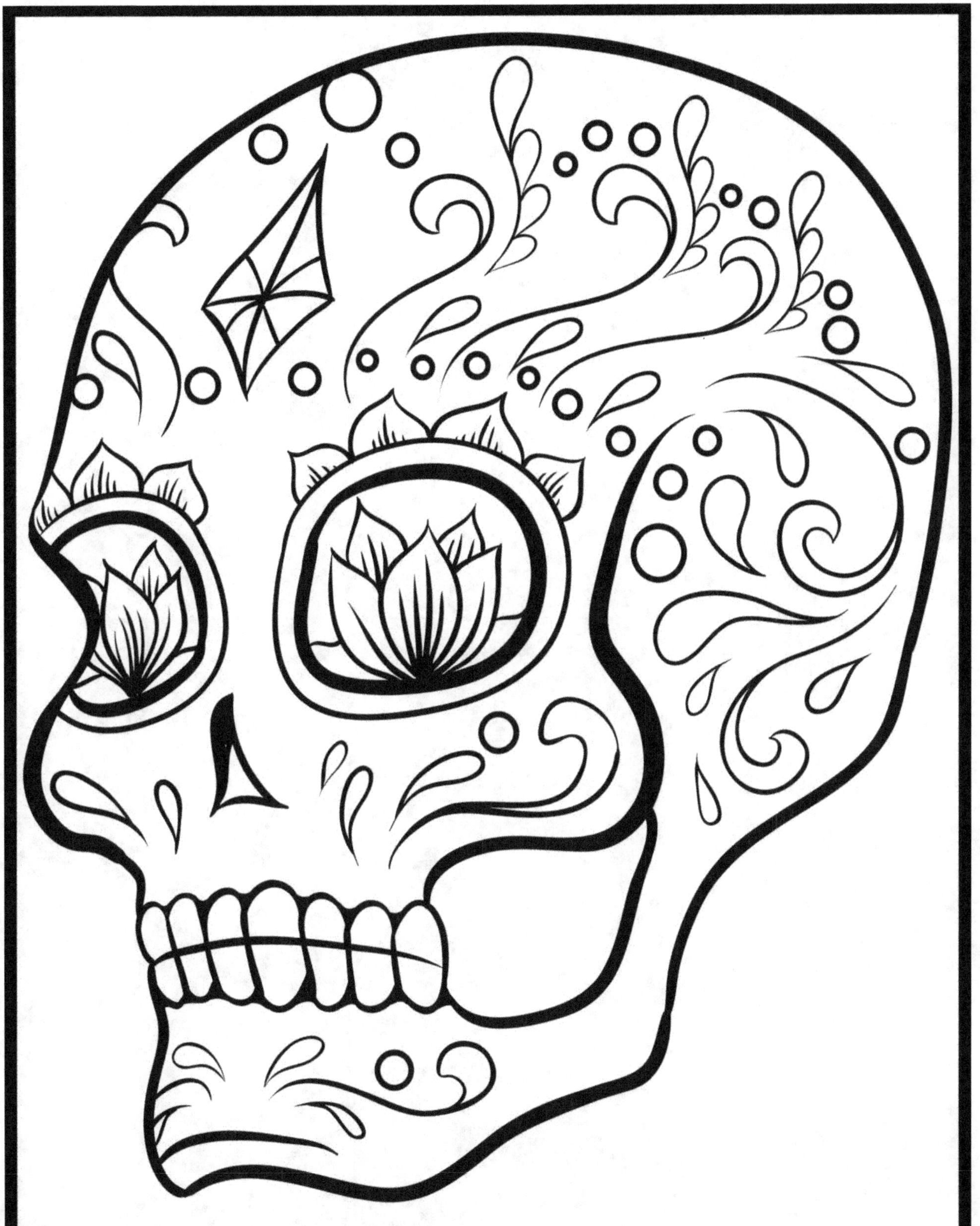

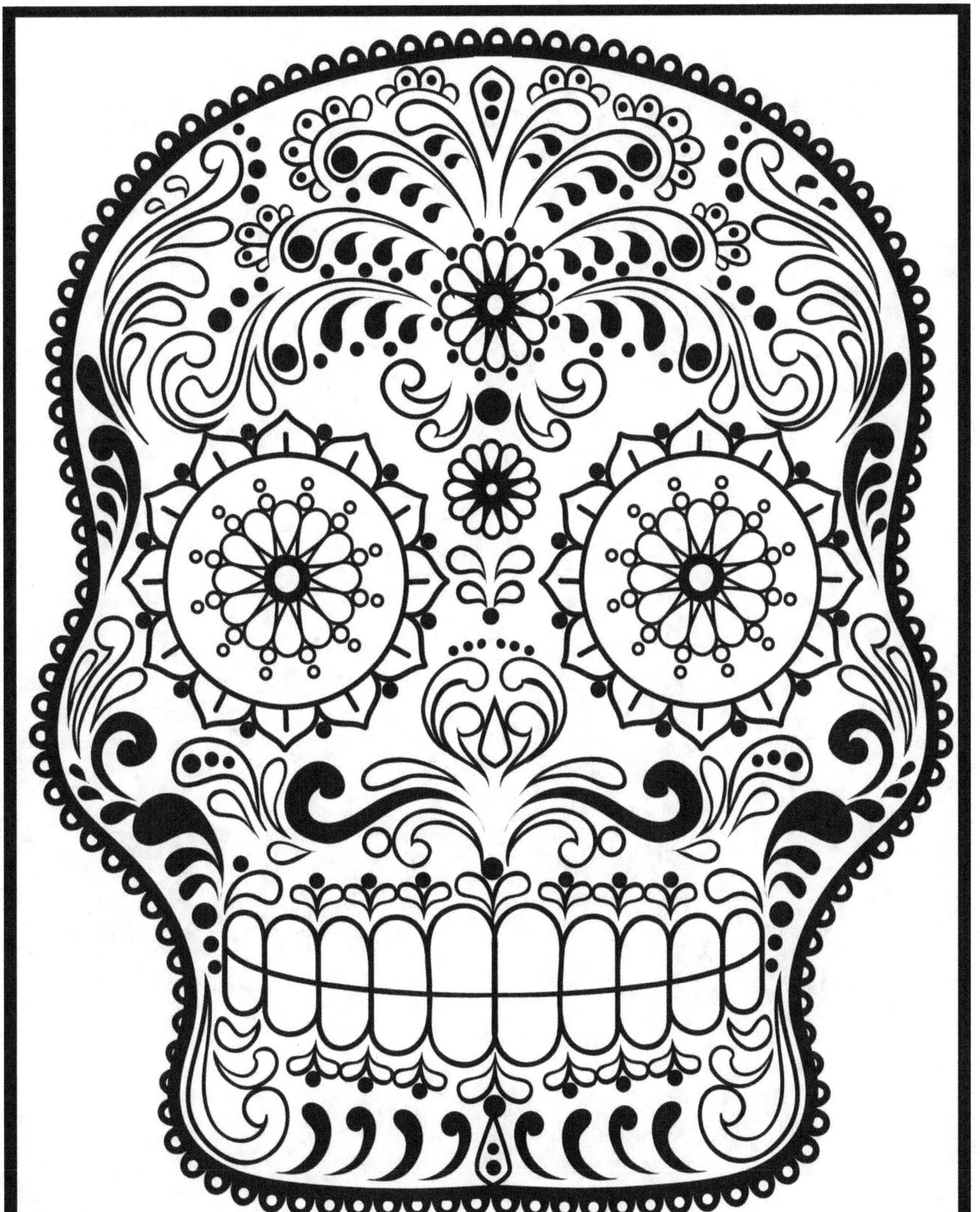

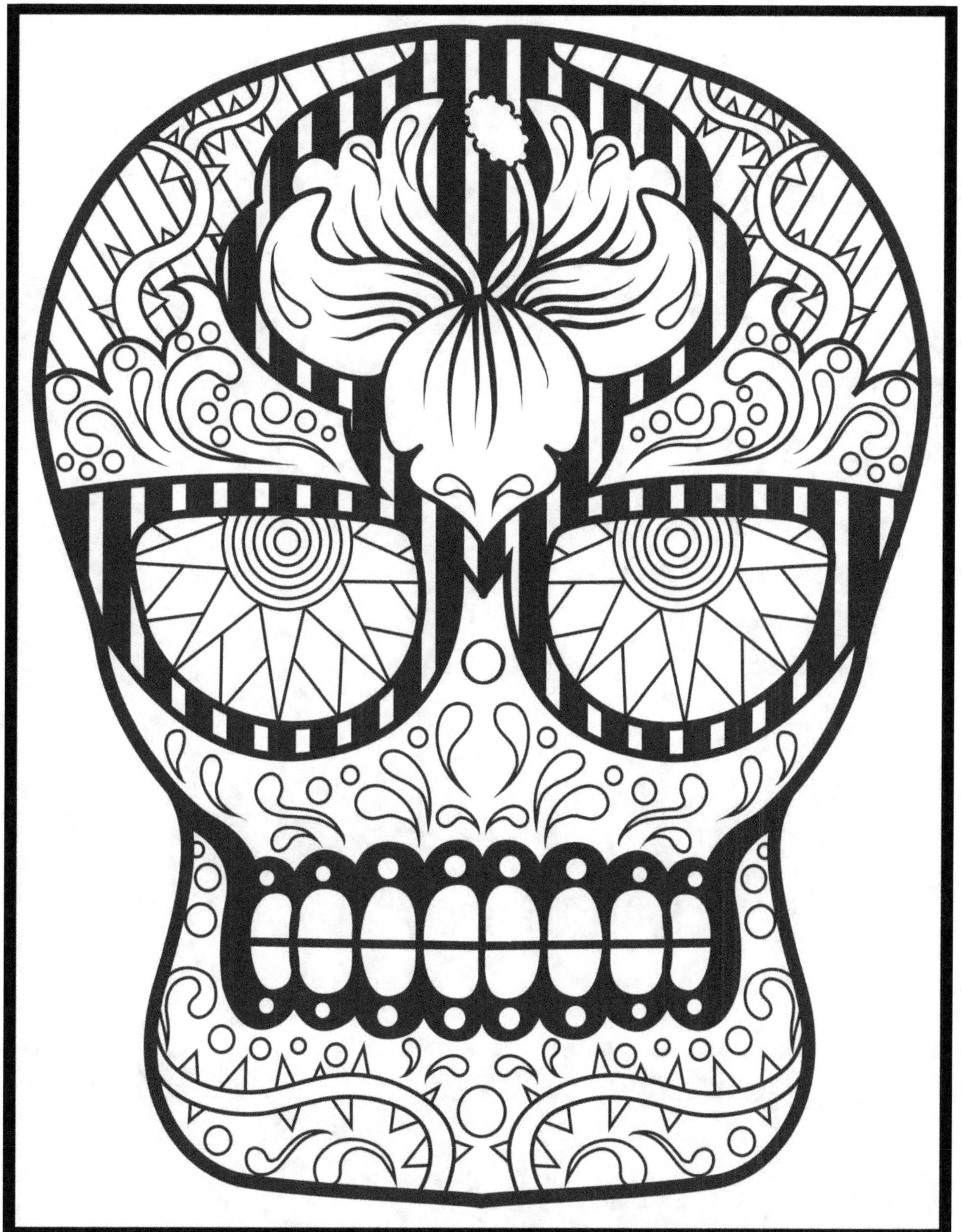

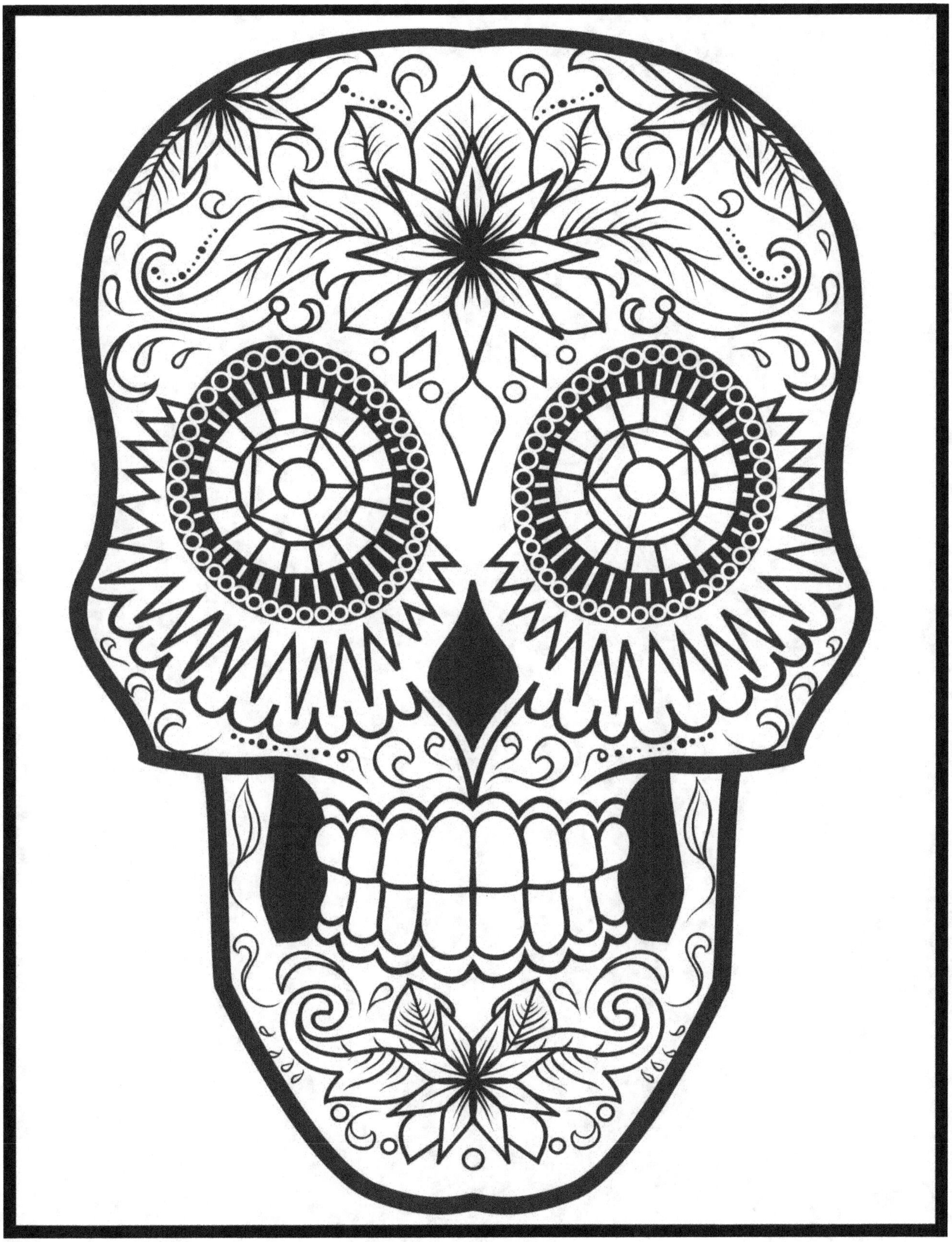

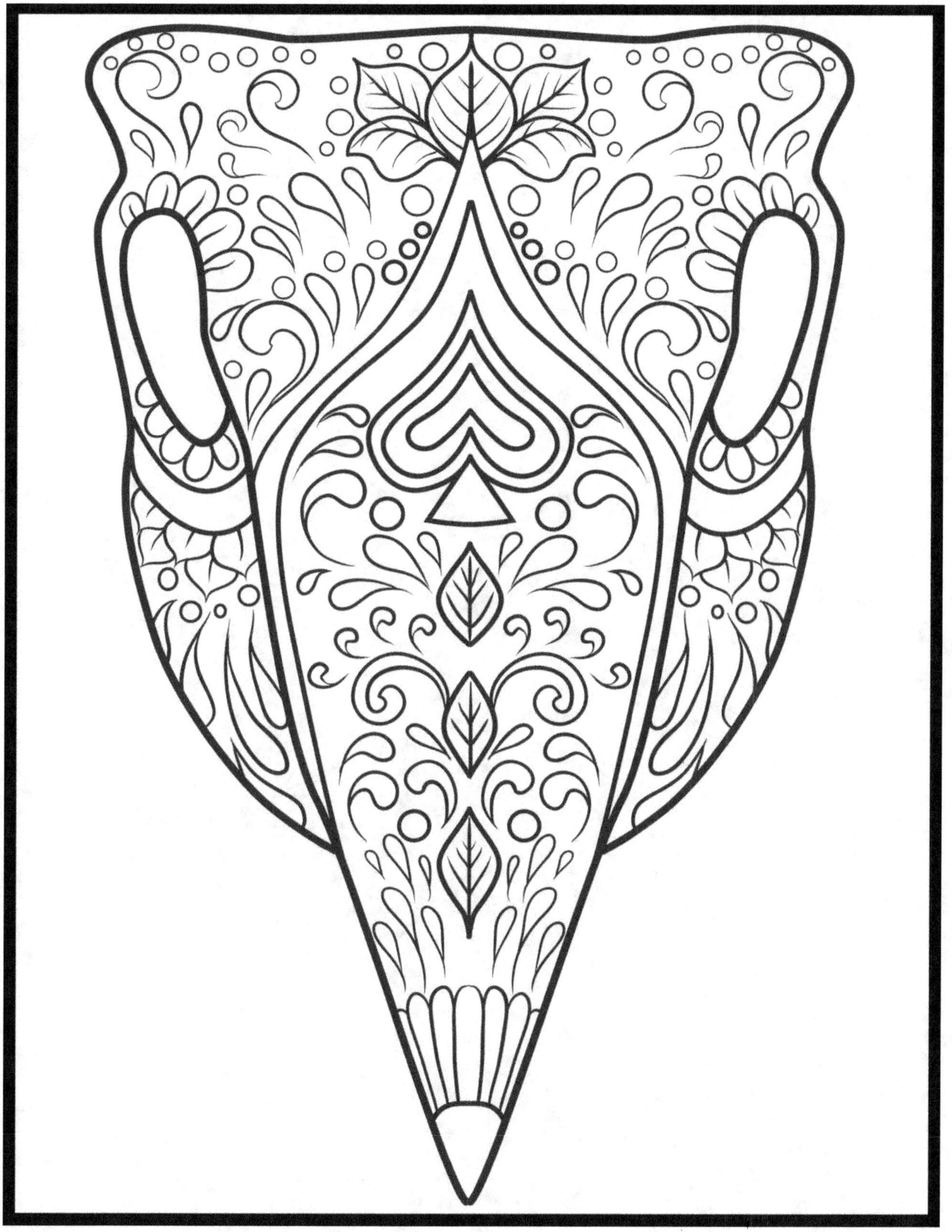

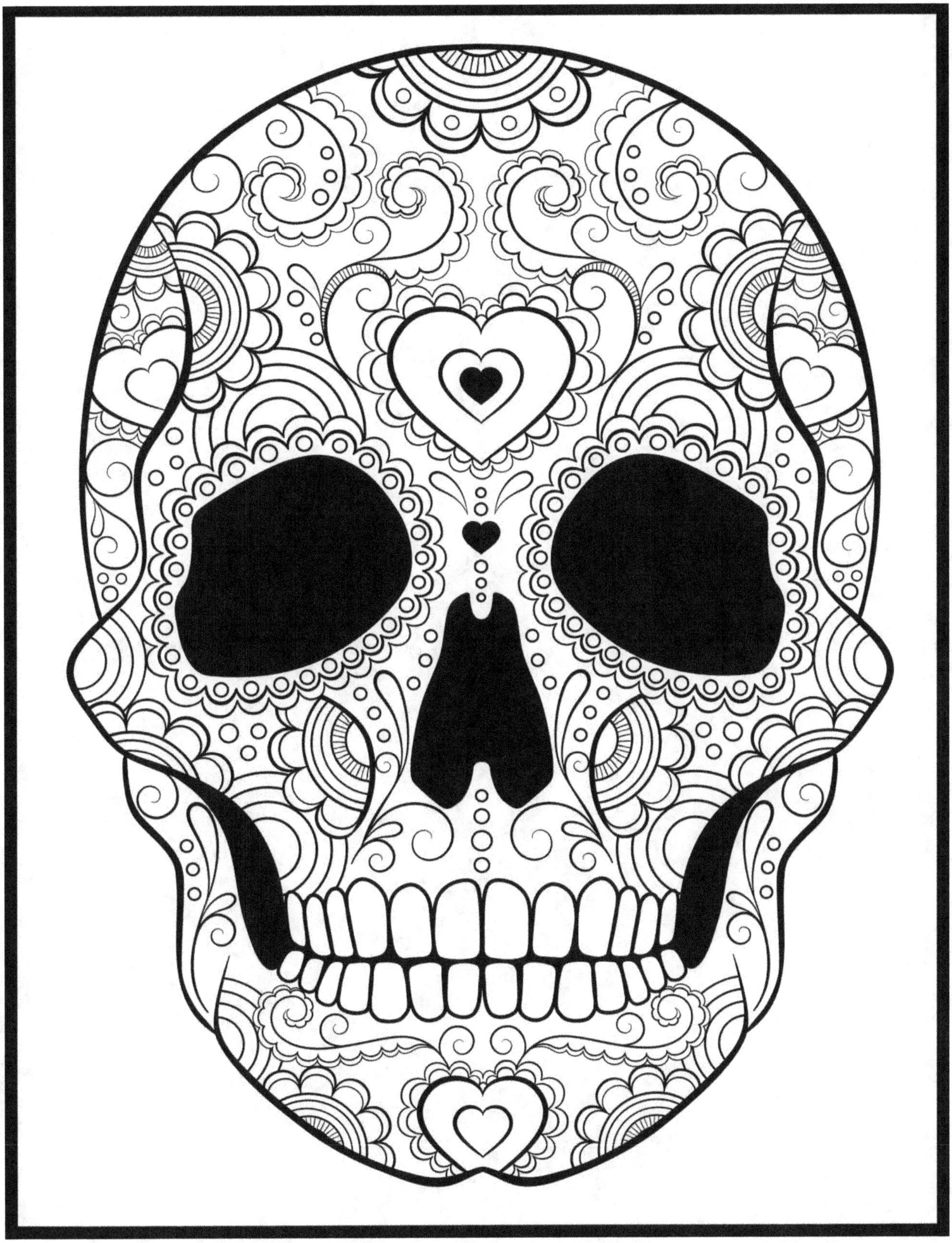

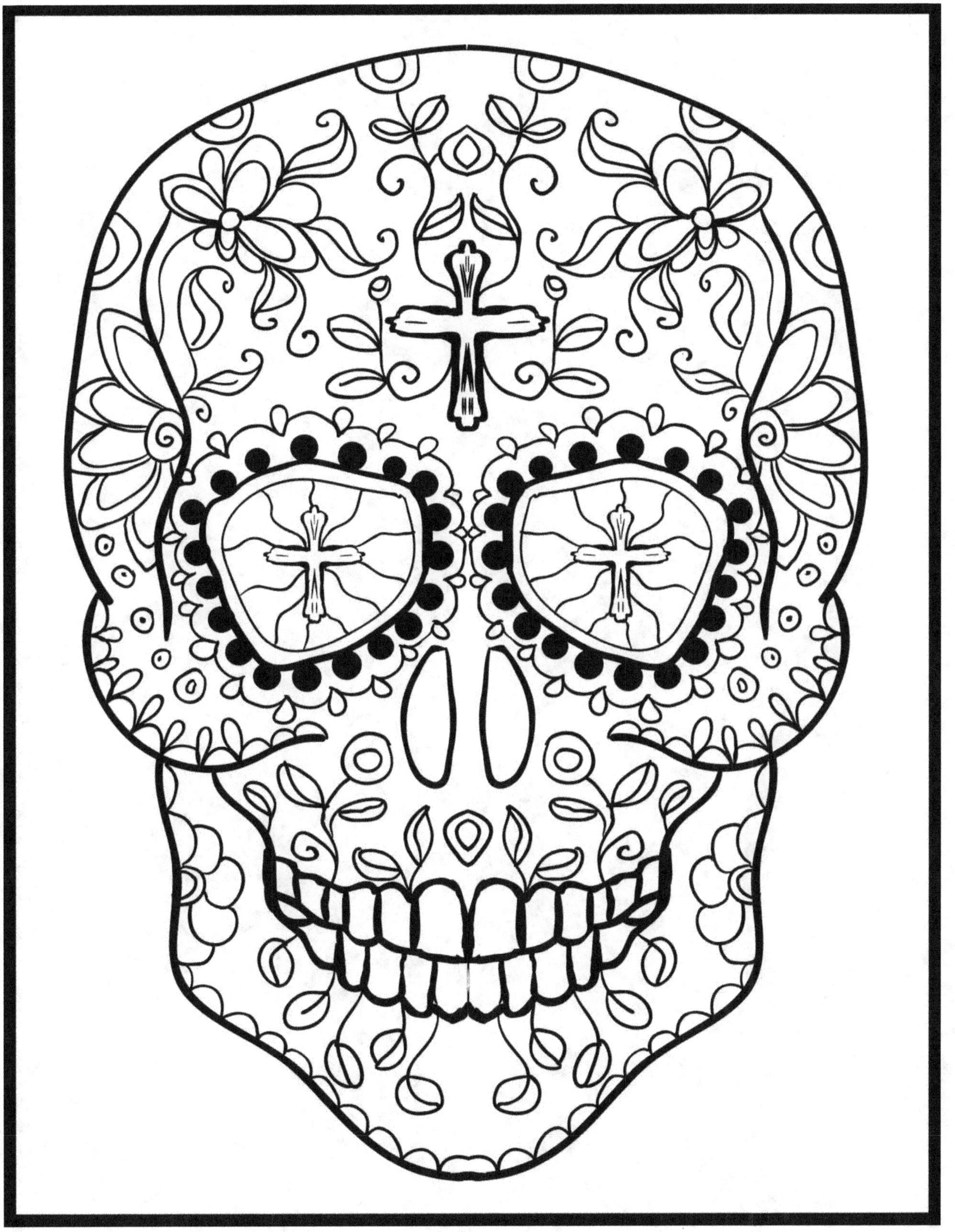

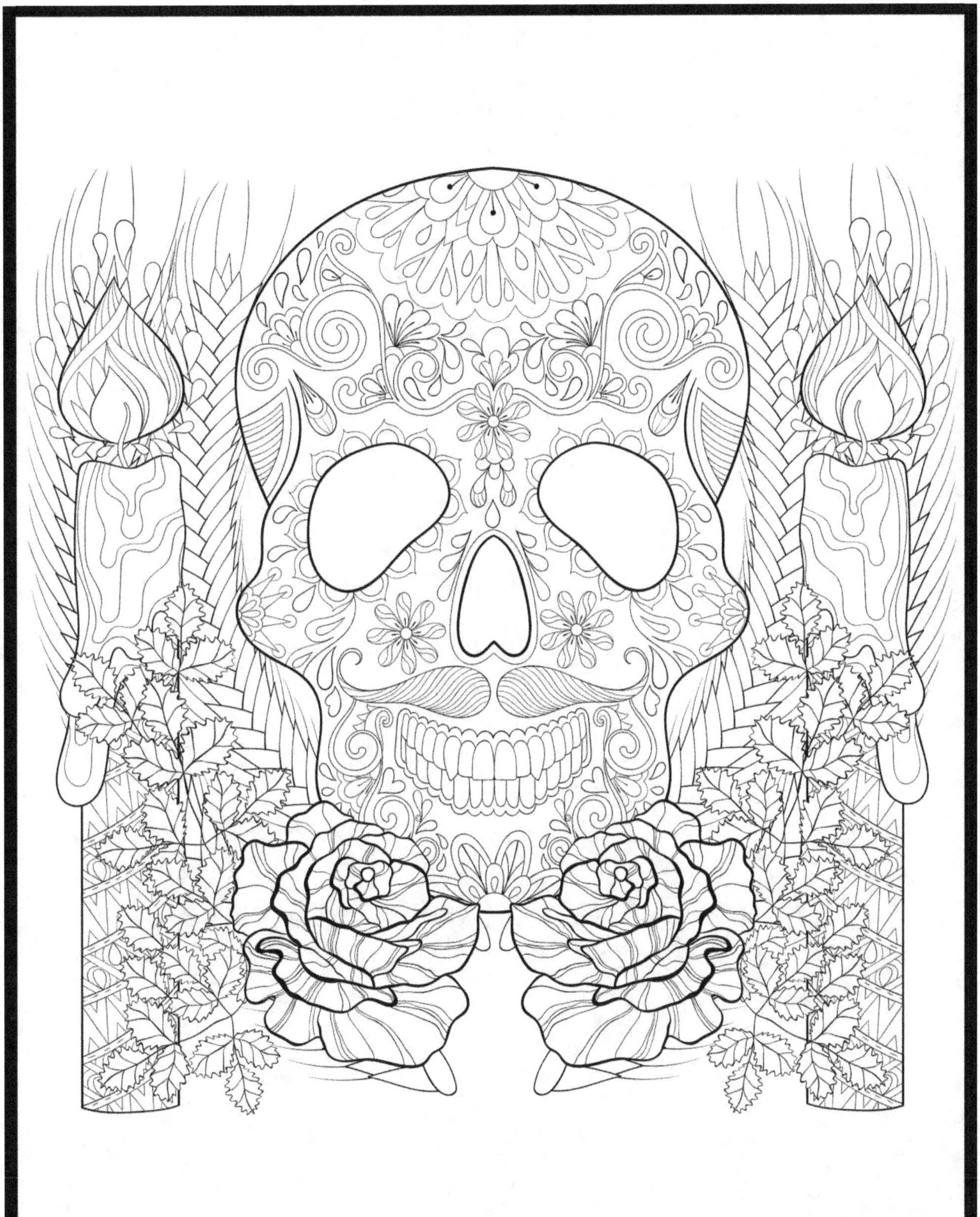

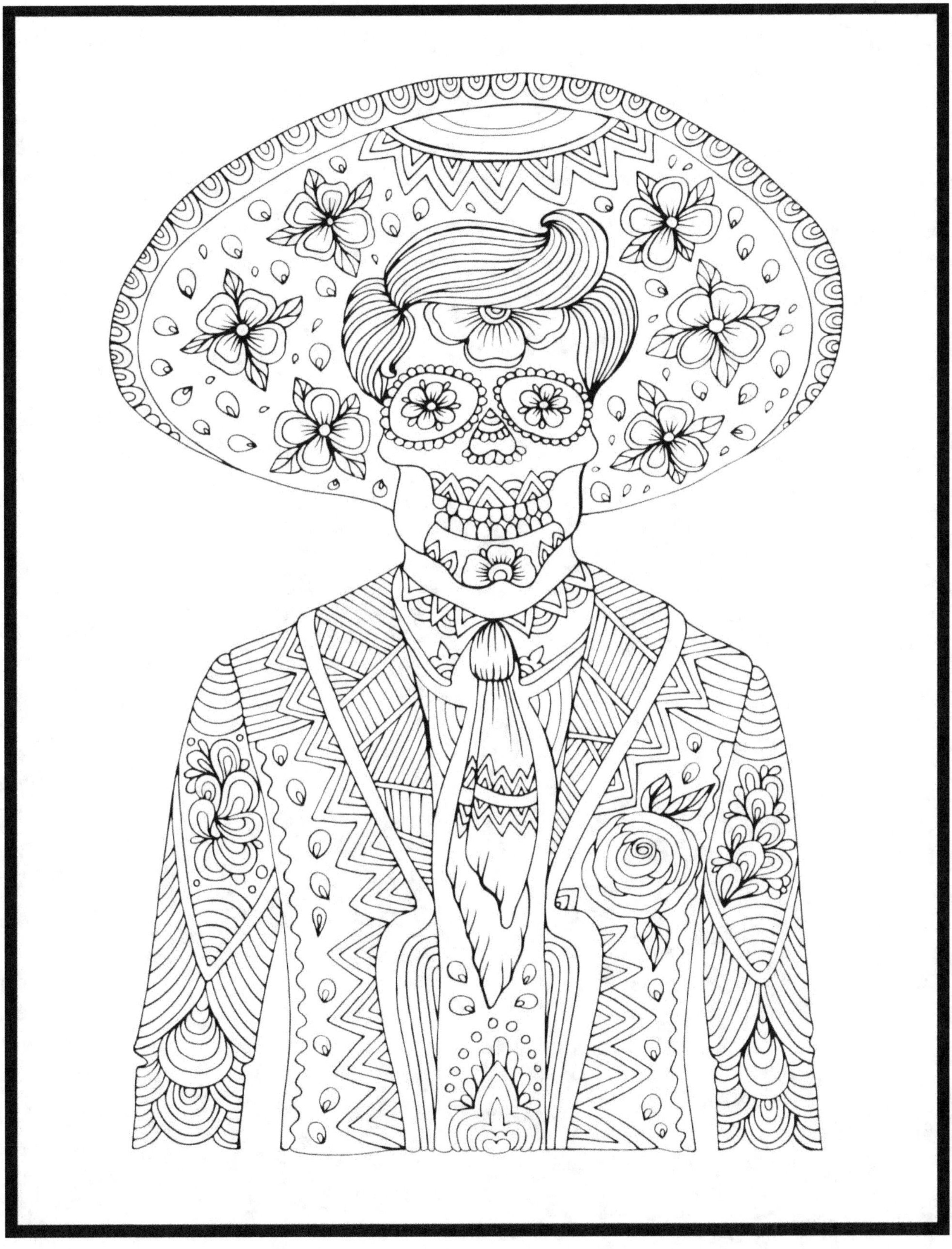

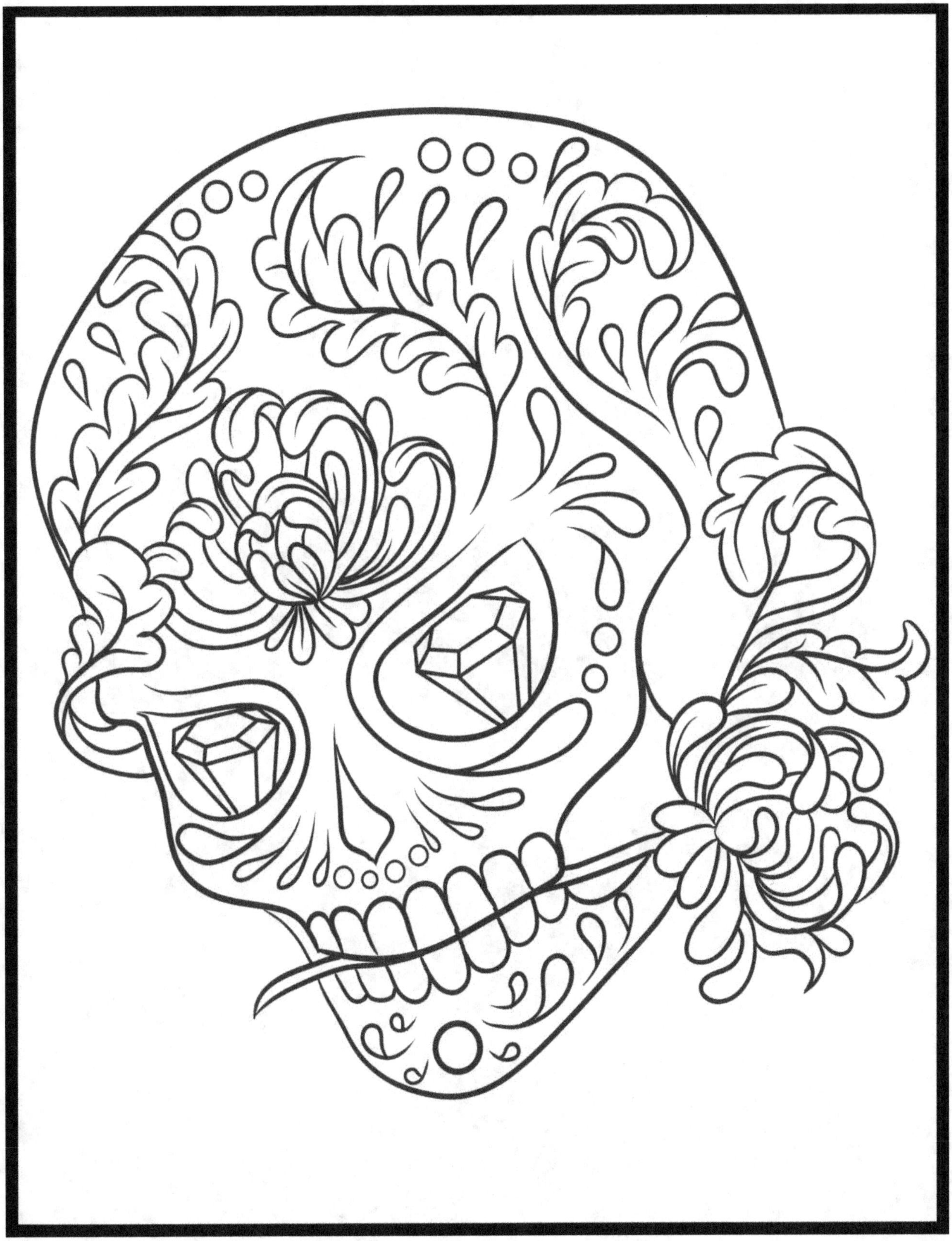

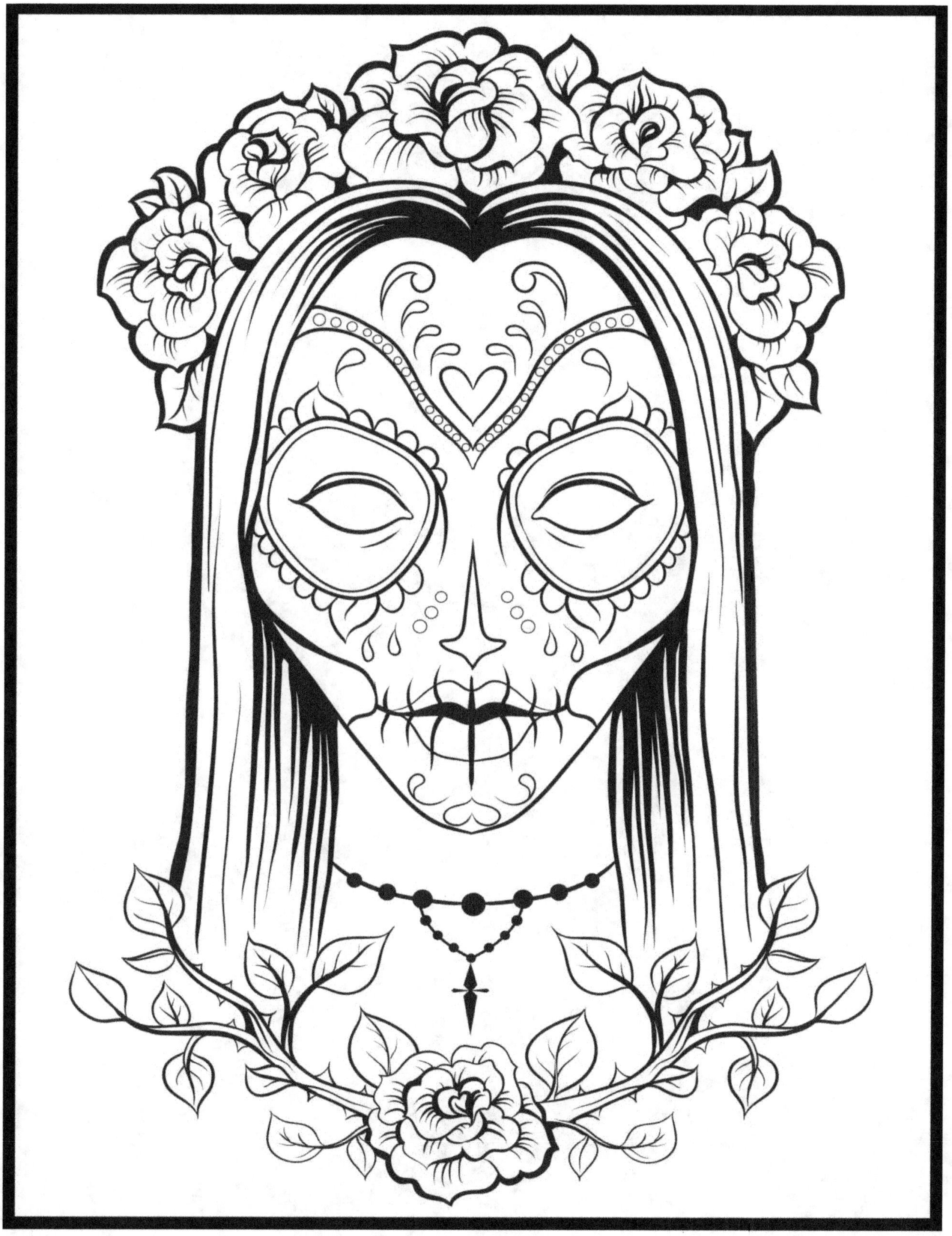

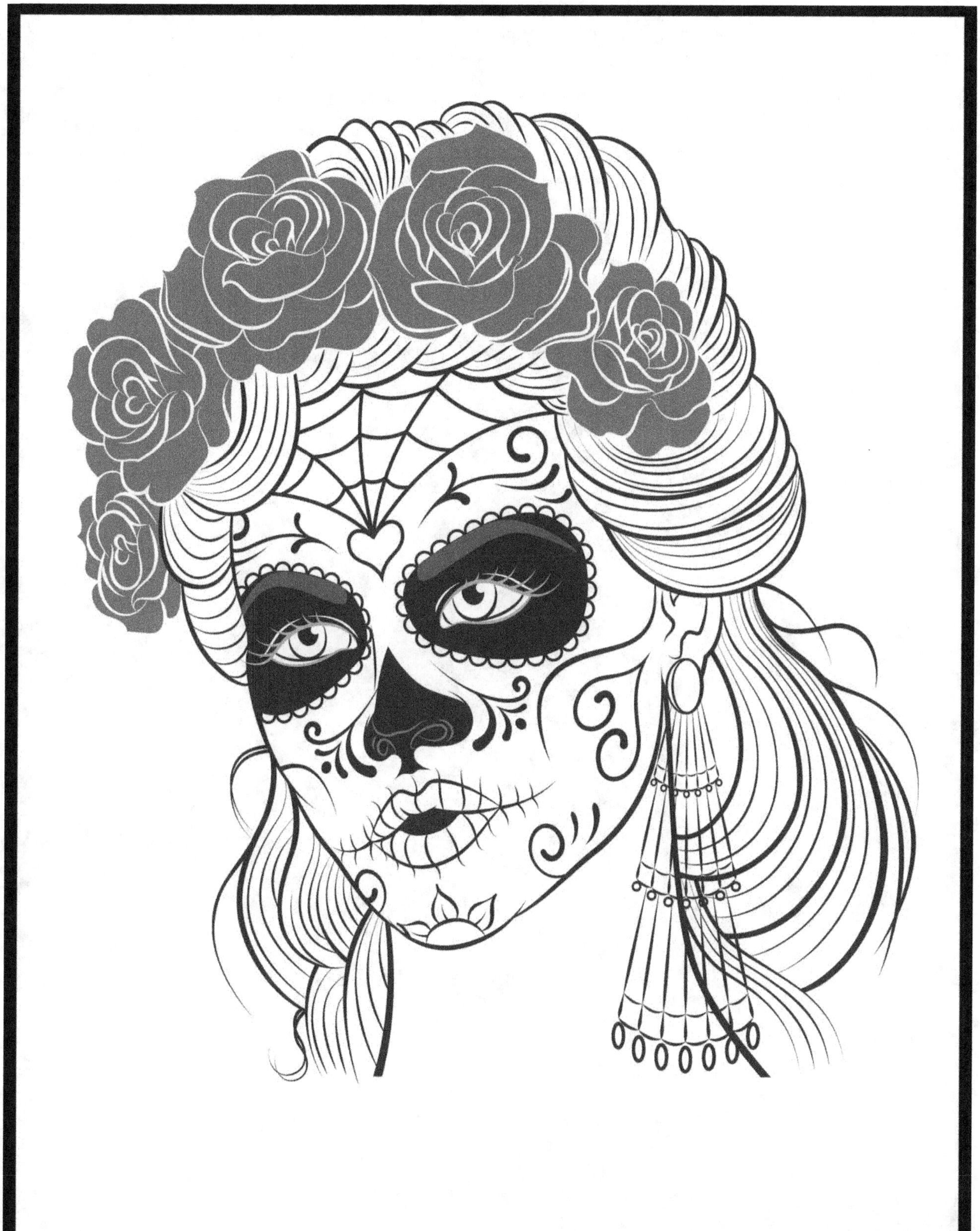

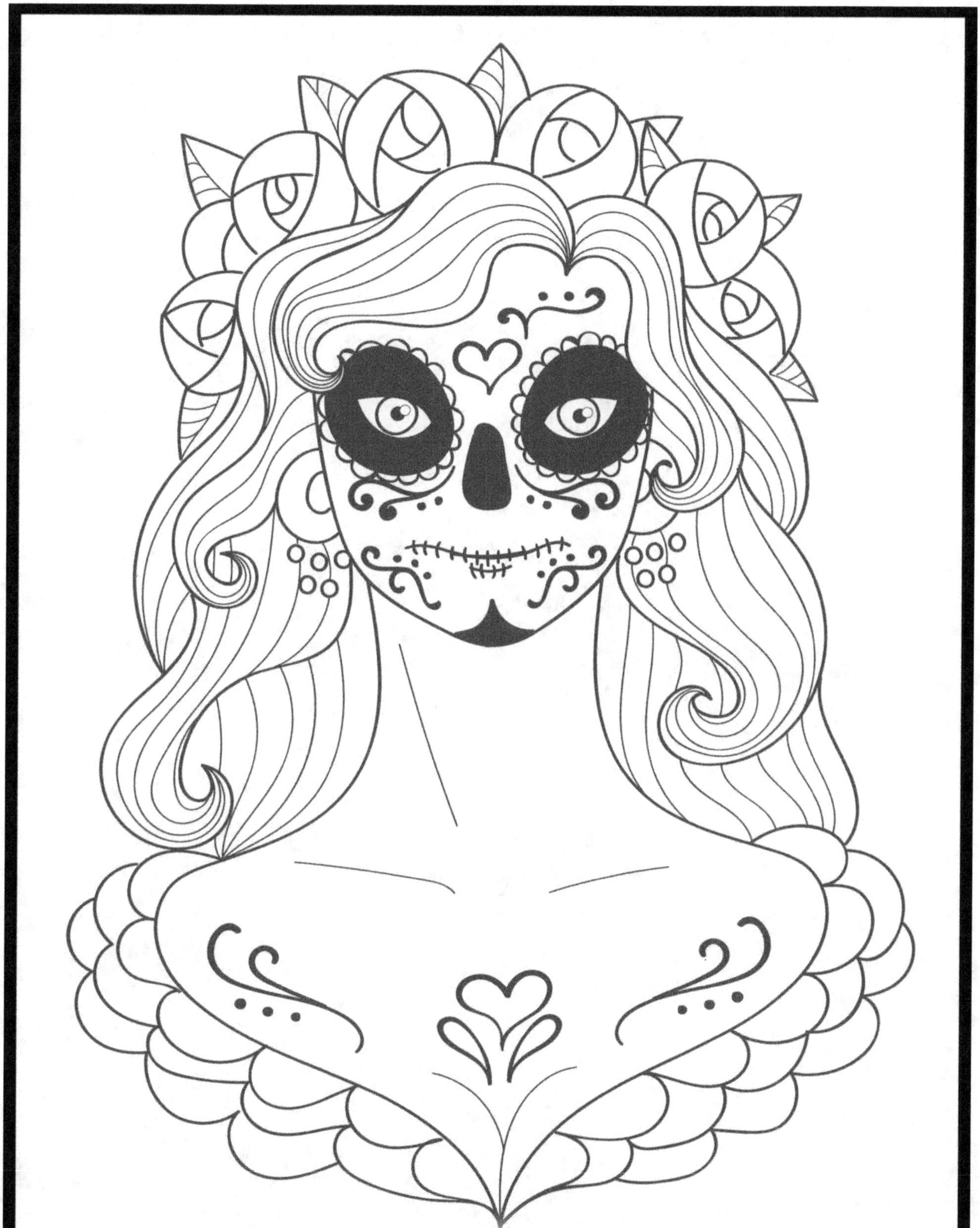

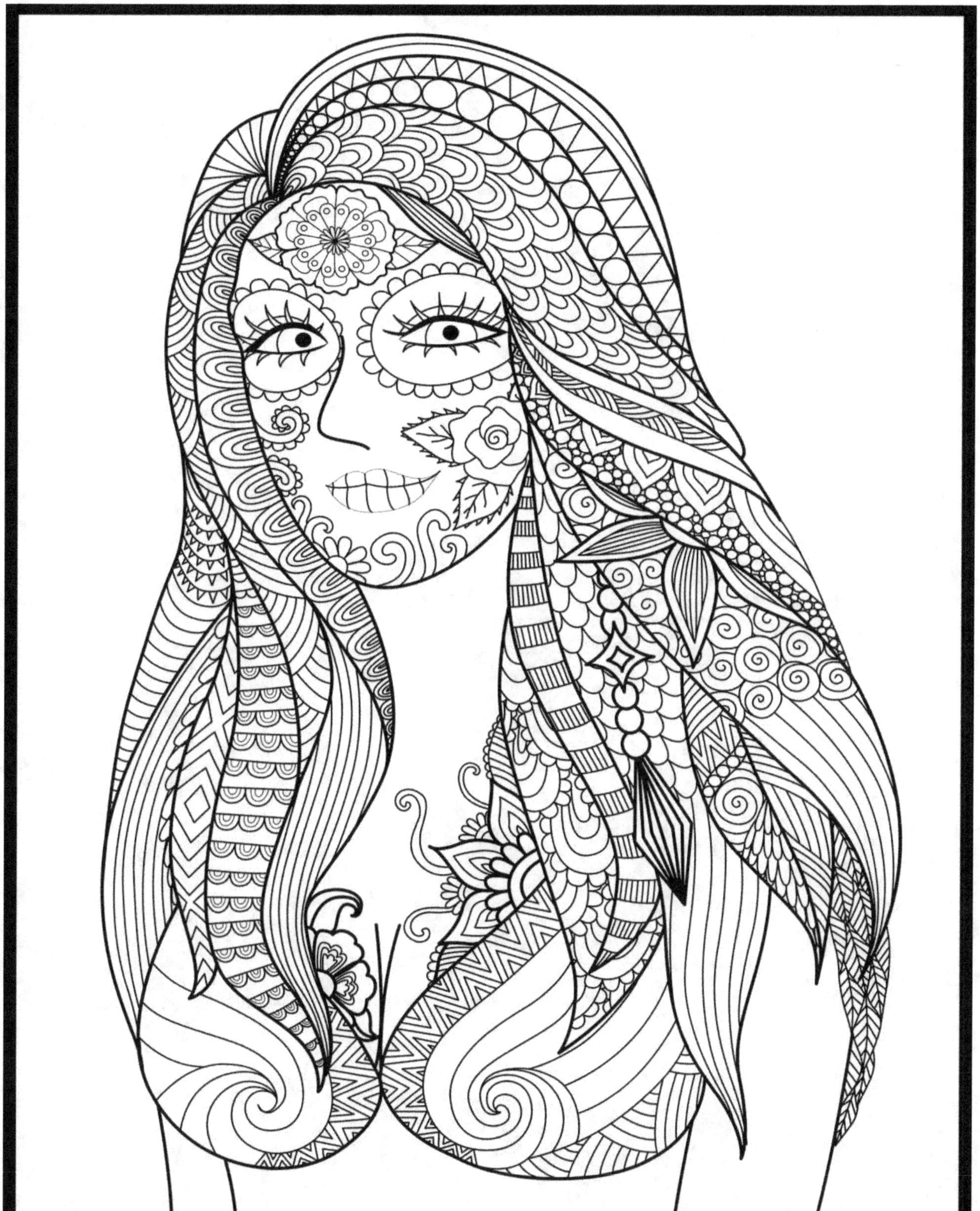

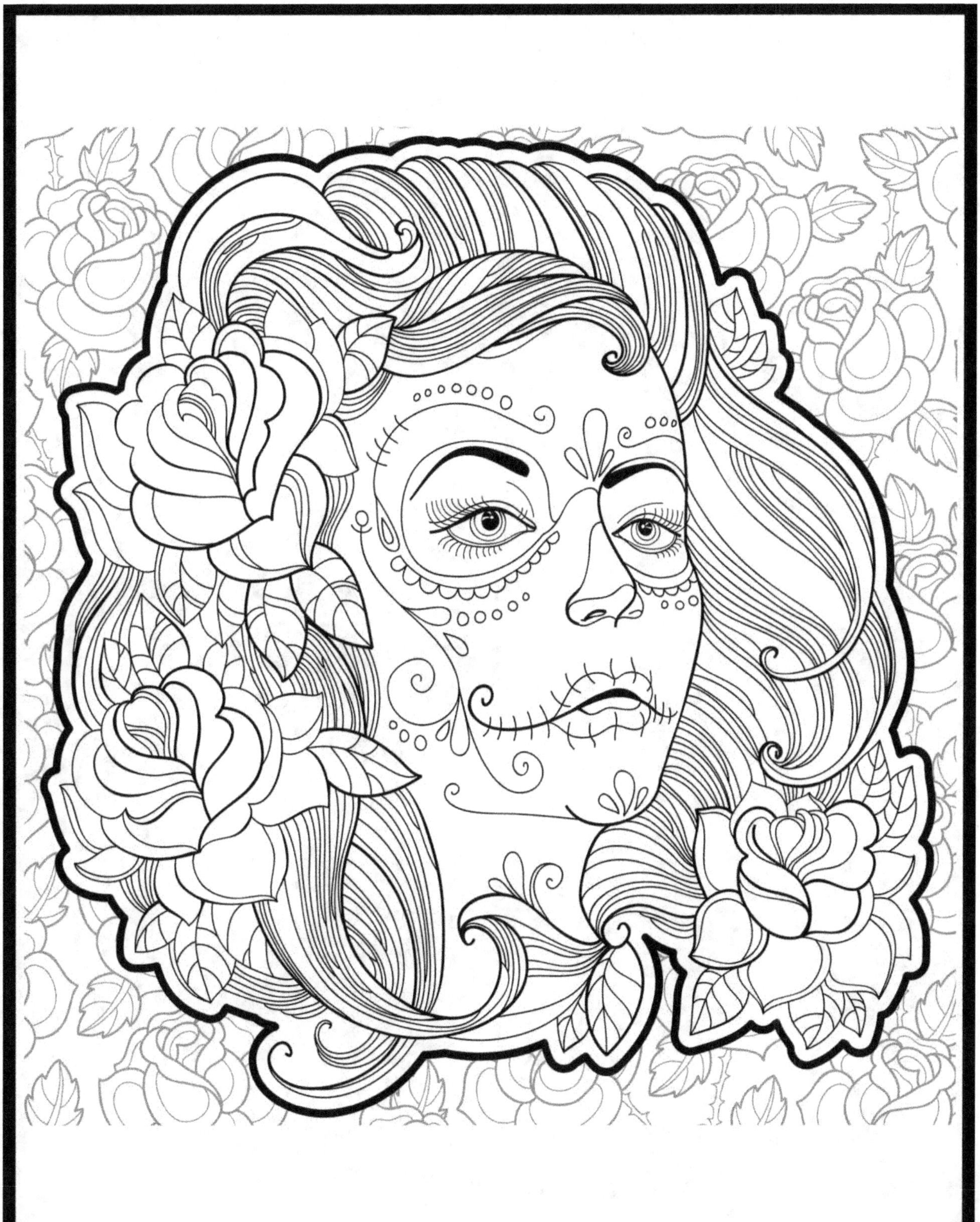

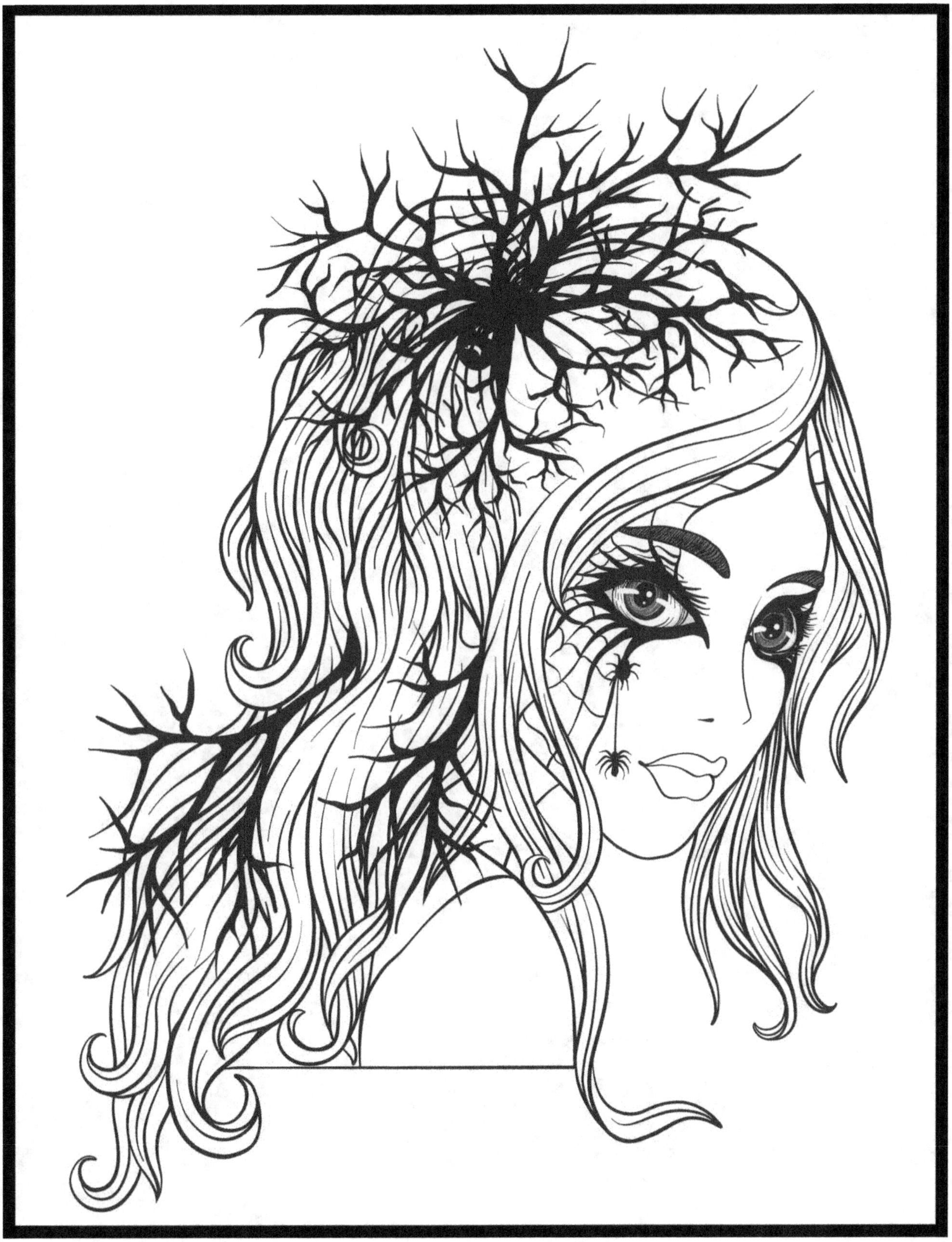

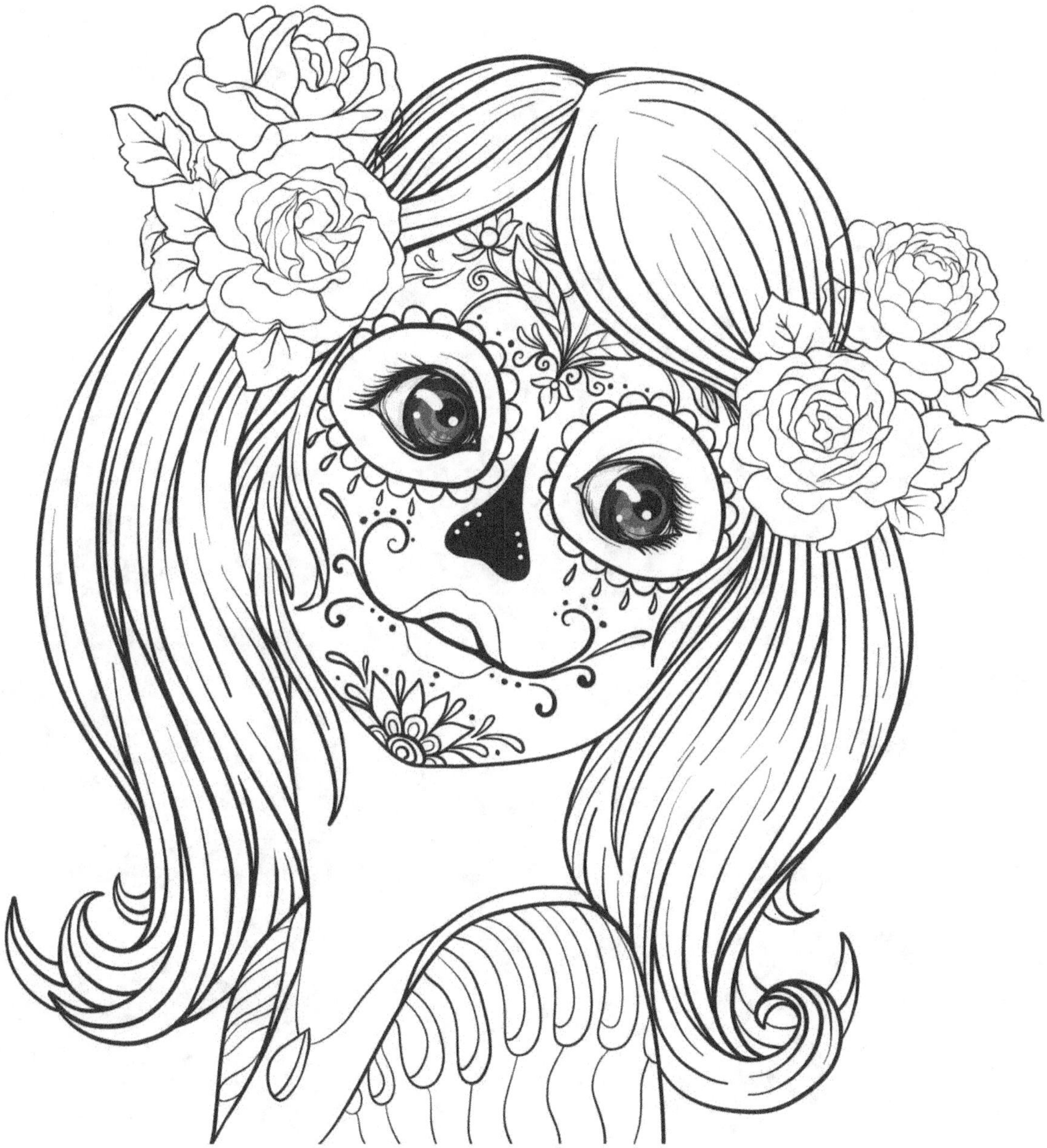

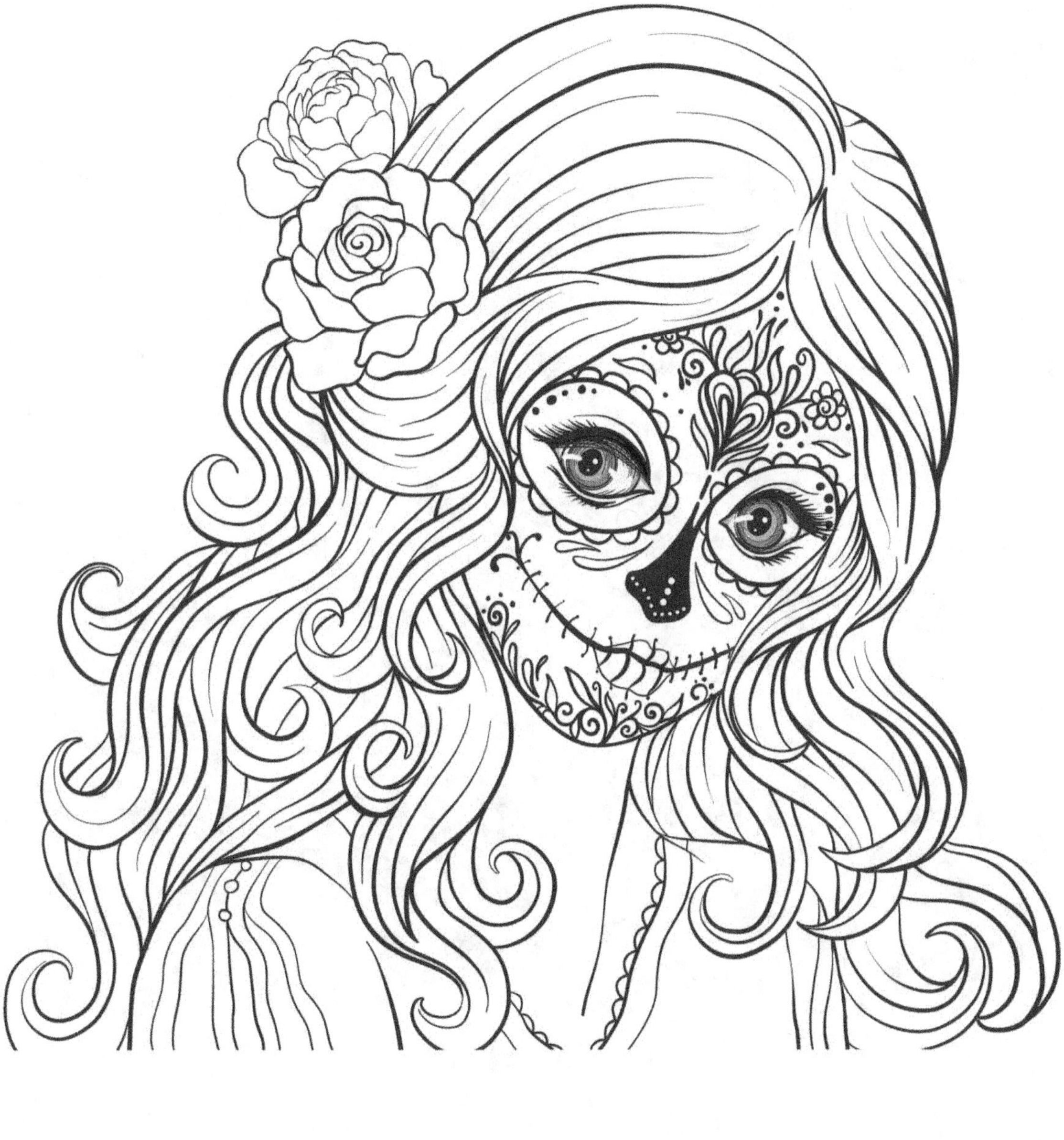

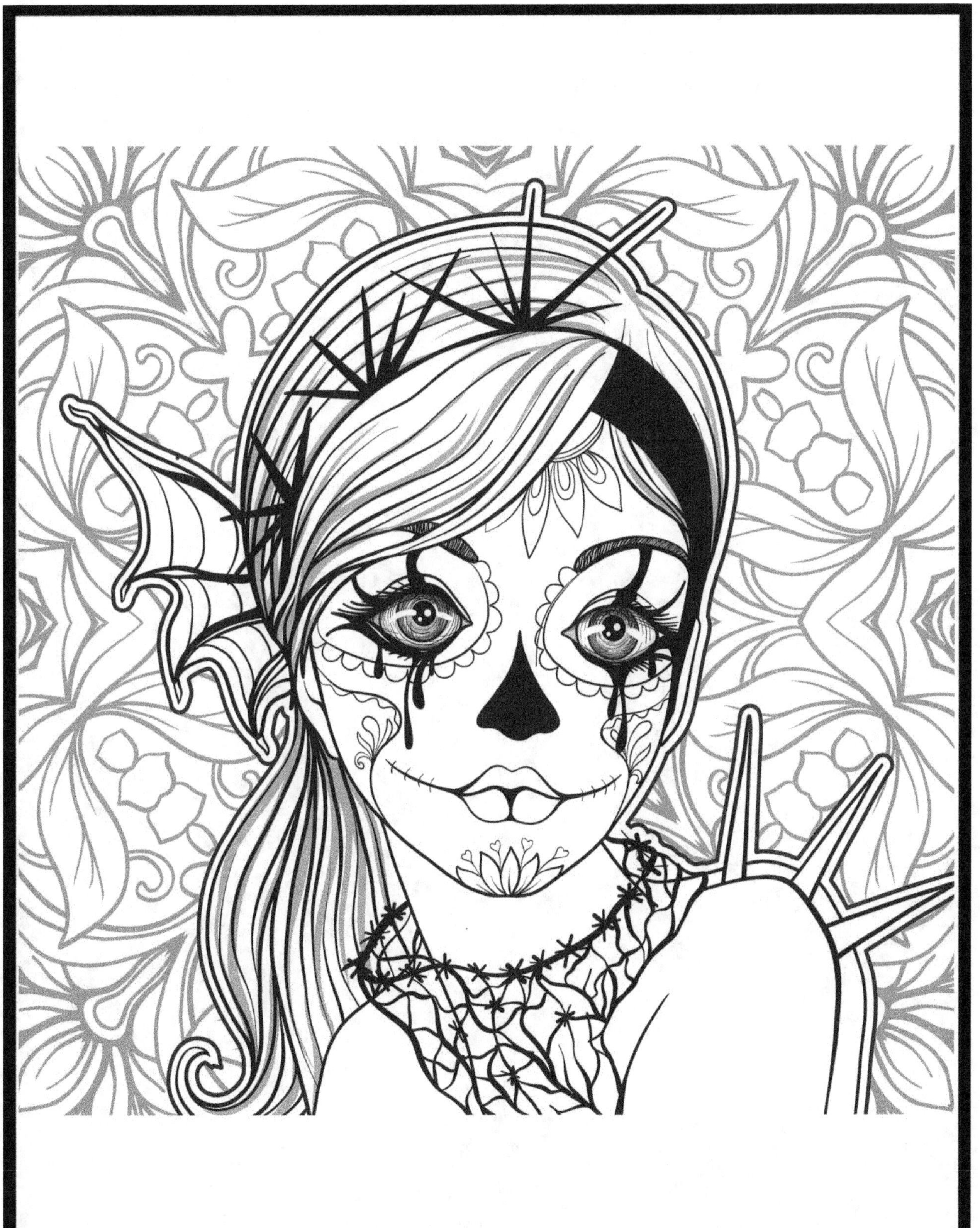

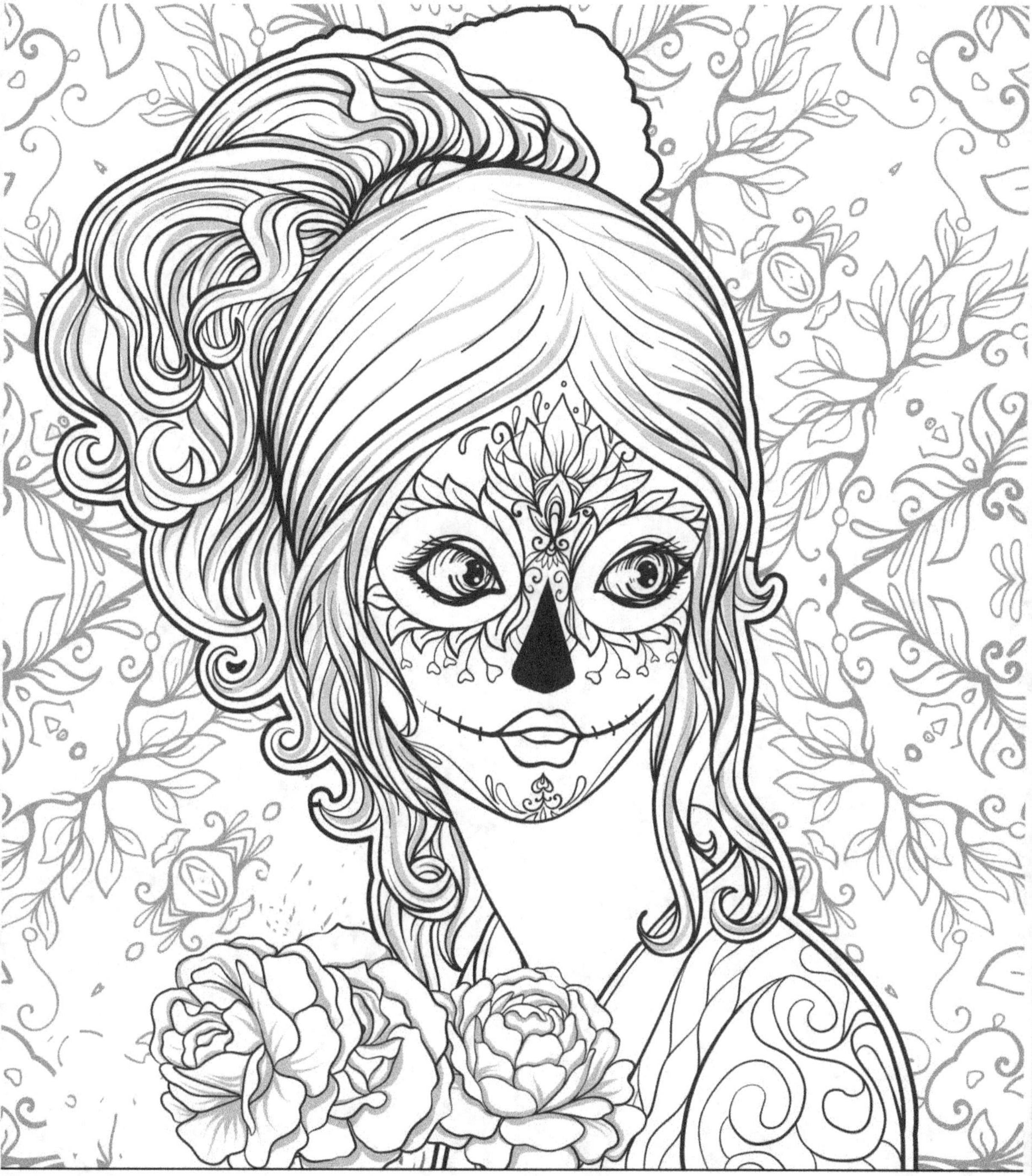

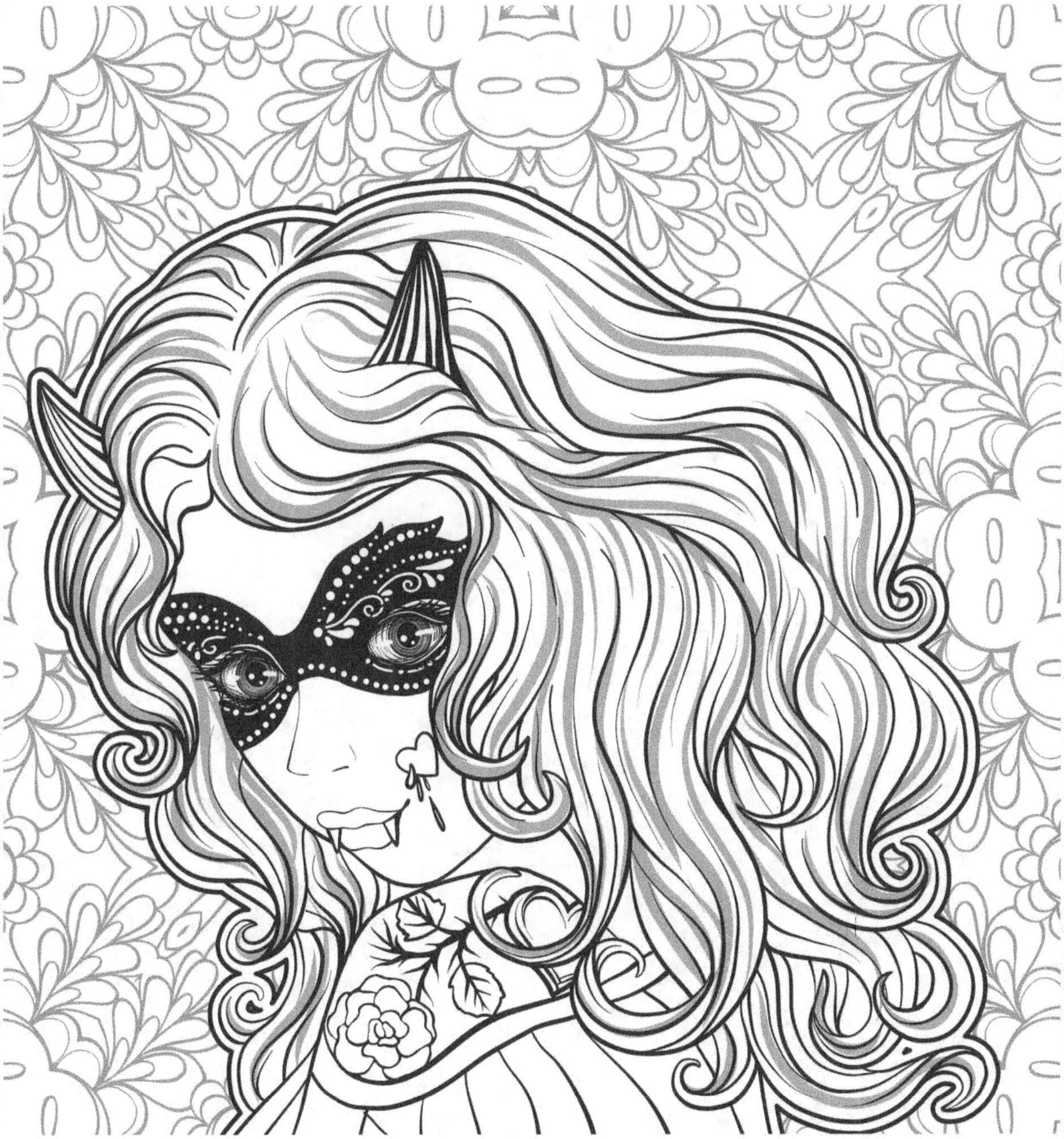

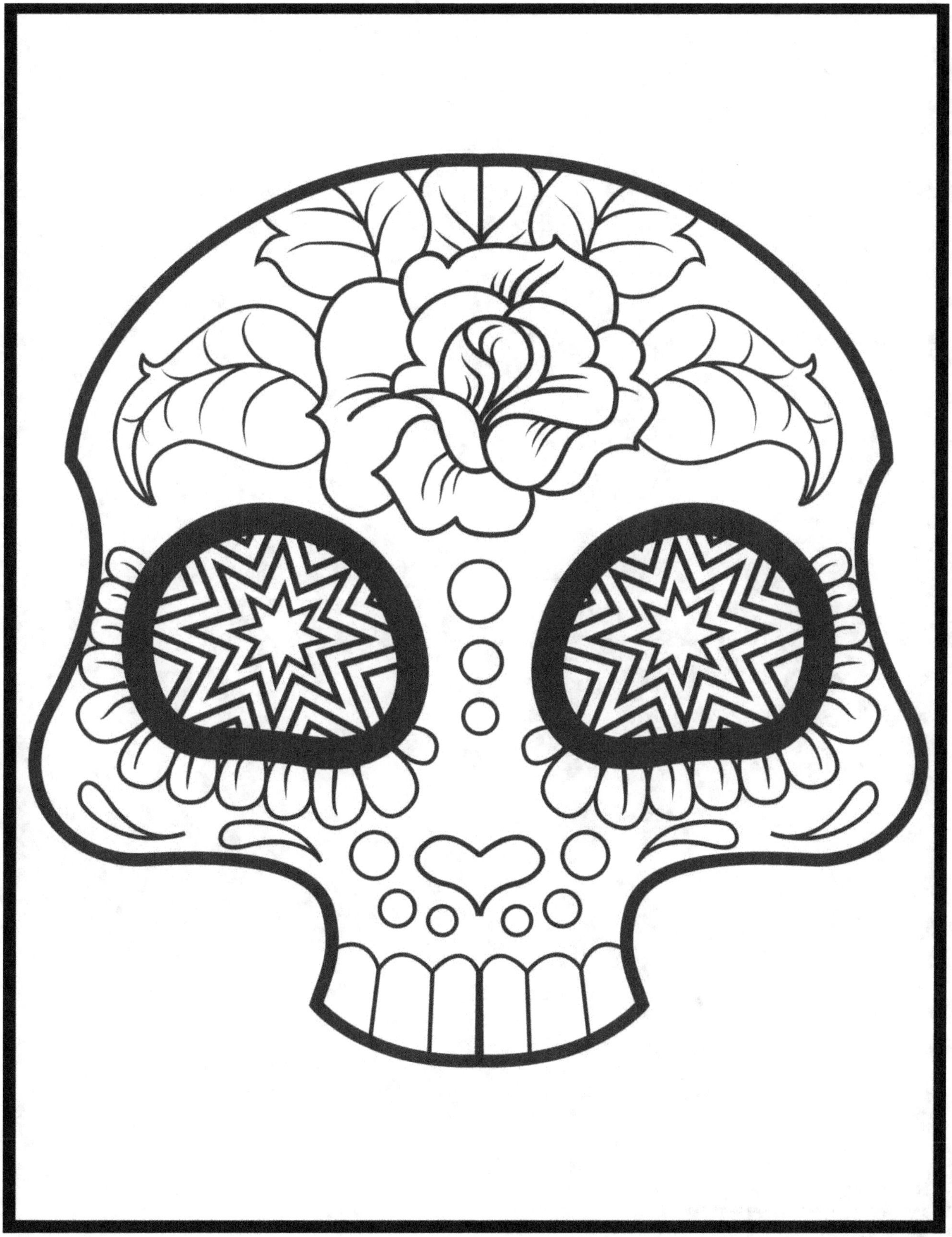

www.ingramcontent.com/pod-product-compliance
Lightning Source LLC
Chambersburg PA
CBHW081607220526
45468CB00010B/2802
* 9 7 8 1 7 2 0 8 0 4 7 4 1 *